Evangelism
That Really
Works

Evangelism That Really Works

John Clarke

First published in Great Britain 1995
Society for Promoting Christian Knowledge
Holy Trinity Church
Marylebone Road
London NW1 4DU

British Library Cataloguing-in-Publication Data
A catalogue record for this book is available from the
British Library

ISBN 0–281–04793–6

Typeset by Wilmaset Ltd, Birkenhead, Wirral
Printed in Great Britain by
The Cromwell Press, Melksham, Wiltshire

To my father Geoffrey, with my sincere thanks for his support for the research project and for all his love over many years.

Contents

Foreword

John Clarke may not be as well known as other names that might come to mind on the subject of evangelism, but I very much doubt whether anyone else will give us a more *useful* book than he has done with this volume.

John Clarke brings three important qualities to this book. First, he has 'a heart for evangelism' – for him it is not an optional extra. Second, he is a 'parish man'. It is a positive qualification for a book on this subject that it comes from someone who daily pounds the beat of a parish. So often guidance on evangelism is sought from those who have extraordinary personal gifts and experience, and what they say often does not transfer into the life of the average parish. This is not the case with this author.

The third quality – and one which makes this book particularly useful – is that John Clarke is a researcher. This book, therefore, is not so much a collection of opinions based on one man's experience, but the reflections of a tidy-minded author based on the lessons being learned by many.

The book is easy to read and the author's obvious enthusiasm is catching. There is a danger, however, that his chatty approach can conceal the very important thinking he presents. He is far more than an enthusiast. He thinks well. He shares with me a strong conviction that churches, not individuals, are the real evangelists. All of us as individuals are called to play our part in the process of helping people discover the gospel, but the life of a congregation is the most powerful agent available. That is why a church must be able to think out and deploy strategies that are likely to lead to people being brought to faith. Most of our churches are set up to teach and nurture those they already have. We need churches that know how to reach and evangelize those who are not yet with us.

He also shares with me the need to work with defined terms in the discussion of evangelism. Strategizing needs a clear set of definitions and terms. John Clarke offers us a set of such terms in this book and it would be good if we all adopted them in our thinking and discussion. Naturally I am flattered to see that he has borrowed some of the terms I have been advocating, but that is not the only reason why I value his work!

This book therefore is not only a useful fund of good ideas, it is an introduction into clear thinking about the evangelistic task. John Clarke is concerned, as we all should be, not for an evangelism that makes a good discussion topic, but for an evangelism 'that really works'. That is exactly what is needed, and if I had the money I would buy a copy for every church in the Diocese I serve!

✠ Gavin Maidstone

Acknowledgements

My sincere thanks are due to all those, mainly
ministers, who have given me their time and help.

PART 1
Understanding the Process

1 Evangelism in Context

'The Church . . . exists in order to evangelize.' The writer was Pope Paul VI.[1] Most catholics, every evangelical, and many liberals would agree. Yet many of us, consciously or unconsciously, are uneasy with evangelism. I believe there are two main reasons.

First, some of us have been put off, either by bad, insensitive evangelism; or maybe by good evangelism which doesn't suit our style. Even if you have a deep respect for Dr Billy Graham, as I do, 'getting them up out'a their seats' may not be for you!

Second, most of us are extremely unsuccessful evangelists. The Churches Together in England Evangelism Research Project[2] reported that the average number of adults publicly professing faith each year in England was only 3.7 per church. As an angler, I know that nothing puts me off fishing as much as a couple of sessions with almost no fish.

I believe we should see *churches* as the fishermen, not ministers or individuals. That is not to deny the value of personal evangelism, or of the gifted preacher-evangelist, but they are part of a larger whole. Catholics have always emphasized the role of the Church, if at times they have underplayed evangelization. My own evangelical tradition has, in the past, put forward too individualized a version of the gospel. In recent years, thankfully, both have moved towards a model of corporate evangelization.

It follows that if churches are failing to evangelize effectively it cannot result simply from a lack of gifting by the minister. I believe one of the main problems is the adoption of inappropriate *strategies*. These can set in motion a vicious downward spiral. 'I've tried evangelism, and it doesn't work.' That has been said to me more than once. The result in each case has been a switch from attempted mission back into maintenance mode, and a grateful appreciation of the occasional fish which swims into the net. Once when I was fishing in Scotland as a teenager, a fish jumped clean out of the water into my rowing boat. If only God would create more fish like that!

Strategies are long term. They are geared to the guts of a church's life rather than the occasional evangelistic foray. The *style* may be upbeat and confrontational, or it may be gentle with little overt sign of what most people mean by 'evangelism'. The right approach will depend on the tradition of the church, the nature of the local community, and the relationship of the church to that community. In each case, though, fish will be coming to the net. Men and women will be finding a meaningful relationship with God and joining his Church.

This book is written out of the conviction that all churches can catch fish. It is the fruit of a 2-year (part-time) research project looking at how British churches of different traditions, in different cultures, are catching many fish. It is packed with case examples. Not all will be relevant to your church or community, but I believe some will be. Most importantly, I believe the underlying processes of evangelism will apply almost everywhere. My prayer is that this book will supply a clearer understanding of those processes, which will help you find a strategy of evangelization which works in your context.

Evangelism and Evangelization

I have already used two terms almost indiscriminately: *evangelism* and *evangelization*. There is great overlap between them. In practice evangelicals tend to use the former, and catholics the latter, regardless of context. William Abraham argues that, historically, their meaning is identical.[3] Nevertheless, many now would define *evangelism* in narrower terms than *evangelization*.

Evangelism has its emphasis on the proclamation of the gospel, and is directed towards the conversion of the individual. The Lausanne Covenant defined it thus:

> to evangelize is to spread the good news that Jesus Christ died for our sins and was raised from the dead according to the Scriptures, and that as the reigning Lord he now offers the forgiveness of sins and the liberating gift of the Spirit to all who repent and believe.[4]

Several writers have argued that this definition is too narrow. Abraham argues that it should include incorporation into the church, that is, nurture and baptism.[5] Most church growth writers would wish to include *presence*, that is, Christian witness and friendship, and also *persuasion*, an awkward term to cover the kind of discussion which takes place in enquirers or adult catechumenate groups. I heartily agree with both, not least for the pragmatic reason that it is usually impossible to separate out proclamation from the other elements in the journey to faith. Words need to be usable! This is developed further in chapter 2.

Evangelization, all are agreed, is broad in its definition. It includes the process leading up to Christian commitment, as well as the period of nurture afterwards. All Christians are in need of further evangelization, in typical Roman Catholic usage of the term. It includes influencing cultures as well as individuals. For example, building a church school could be described as an act of evangelization, but scarcely of evangelism. 'For the Church, *evangelizing* means bringing the good news into all the strata of humanity, and through its influence, transforming humanity from within and making it new . . .'[6]

Is this book about *evangelism* or *evangelization*? The truth is, it is somewhere in between. Its central theme is really the social processes by which people are drawn into contact with the Church and to faith in Christ. Its concern is therefore much broader than the narrow (Lausanne Covenant) definition of *evangelism* above, but it is limited to the activities of the local church, and therefore more restricted than many definitions of *evangelization*. Will the reader forgive me if, on occasions, I use the terms almost interchangeably?

Maybe I should give my own definition of evangelism. It is far from perfect, but at least it may clarify what this book is about:

> Evangelism *involves a subtle process of human interaction. Through it, men and women experience God's love, expressed by his people, and come to hear and understand the truth of the gospel. The Holy Spirit is at work in all this, often in ways we do not understand. As a result, people start to follow Christ and join his church.*

Opposition to Evangelism

The central theme of this book is that every church needs an effective strategy for evangelization. In my experience there are four sources of opposition to this idea.

First, there are some liberals who are opposed to the very idea of evangelism on the basis of deeply held theological convictions. My impression is that such folk are fairly few and far between. If you are one of them I can only say I disagree with you passionately, but I respect your views, and I'm delighted you still bought this book!

Second, and I believe far more numerous, are those liberals and catholics who broadly speaking accept the *principle* of evangelization, but find it a turn-off in *practice*. They believe that the scene has been hijacked by evangelicals and charismatics like me! I am optimistic that I can persuade you that catholic, evangelical, and even liberal approaches to evangelism are, in fact, converging. I believe you will find that most of the case examples in this book are relevant across churchmanship, sometimes with a little adaptation.

Third, there are a few of my fellow evangelicals – sometimes charismatics, occasionally Calvinists – who consider the very idea of strategy or planning to be somehow unspiritual. The *Lord* should lead us into evangelism, and we shouldn't need to think about it very much. One vicar told me that the growth of his church was due to the sovereignty of God, nothing more, nothing less, and there were no conceivable lessons that anyone else could learn from it. Actually, he did say that the church had recently hit some problems, but I did not dare ask whether these were also due to the sovereignty of God!

I find this view in its extreme form ridiculous, but put more moderately I believe it needs to be taken seriously. Is there a risk of our relying on social theory and management technique rather than on the power of God? I acknowledge that there *is* such a risk. Nevertheless, prayer and analysis need not be alternatives. Each should, and can, inform and strengthen the other. May I leave the point for now? I shall take it up again in the final chapter.

Fourth, and more surprisingly, gentle opposition can be experienced from some in the church growth school. The argument here is that evangelism is valid, but not usually the key issue. Using a biological model of the Church, based either on St Paul or Jesus' parables of the kingdom, they will argue that a healthy church will automatically grow. If a church is not naturally growing and making new disciples there is something wrong with it. It is either sick or dead. The key issue, therefore, is not finding an effective evangelism strategy, but finding and putting right the problems in the church.

Evangelism, Church Growth and Mission Audit

This last argument from the Church Growth school needs fleshing out, for it is vitally important. There is no doubt that the model of a biological organism is a powerful one for describing the local congregation. It fascinates me that secular writers on organizations have now caught up with it, 2,000 years after Paul!

Roy Pointer[7] and others have suggested that there are factors in church life which lead to growth, and others which lead to stagnation and decline.

One list of growth factors is as follows:

- positive leadership
- agreed agenda
- inspiring worship
- cultural relevance
- use of 'life cells' (home groups)
- training
- spontaneous witness
- planned evangelism
- community involvement
- enabling structures
- believing prayer
- life-related Bible teaching

Lists of 'ailments' which retard growth tend to focus on prevalent attitudes in the congregation such as:

- maintenance complex
- 'fellowshipitis' (being too inward looking)

but also more practical constraints such as:

- inadequate management structure
- overcrowding

The underlying philosophy is as important as the choice of the individual factors. This is that a healthy church will grow, and that, to facilitate growth, one should therefore look at the church's overall life to ensure it is healthy, and take corrective action where appropriate.

This is also the philosophy behind the taking of a 'mission audit' of a local church, which frequently makes use of 'tools' developed by Pointer and others. It is usually 'overall health'-based rather than evangelism-based, though evangelism may be one of the areas considered. This approach regards the church as an organism. Each area of its life depends on the rest of the 'body', and therefore the way to growth is to look objectively, preferably with the help of an unbiased consultant from outside, at all the key areas in a church's life. Involve the congregation in discussion and prayer, make recommendations for change in each area, and hopefully growth will follow.

Let me say that I endorse this approach wholeheartedly, as long as it recognizes that evangelism is *one* of the areas which needs to be considered. It is not always the priority area, but it can be. We shall see that a church can be broadly healthy – and, let us face it, no church is perfect – and still not grow if, for example, it does not have an adequate bridge into its community. If I have any criticism of 'mission audit', it is that it is better at identifying the problems than at finding the solutions. My prayer is that this book will help point to some solutions in the particular area of evangelism.

How are we to decide, then, whether evangelism is an area of priority in a given church? I believe that much depends on the position the church has reached in its growth cycle. This can be expressed as an 'S' curve.

The 'S' Curve

Many churches' growth follows a common pattern. The 'S' curve is shown in figure 1. The first phase is some kind of spiritual renewal. Without spiritual life there can be no growth. In some cases this life can bring significant growth of itself, though it is usually transfer growth – Christians joining from elsewhere. This can be most dramatic in city churches surrounded by large populations, particularly if highly mobile

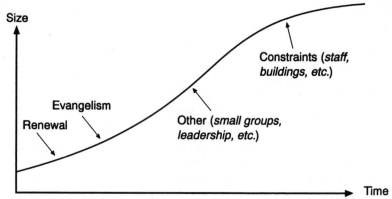

Figure 1 · The 'S' Curve of Church Growth

'receptive groups' such as students or young professionals are involved.

The next phase is where finding a culturally relevant means of evangelism is critical – though usually far from easy. The church has no history of successful evangelism. It is often cut off from its surrounding community. Some kind of 'bridge' has to be found with at least one sector of the community. The particular bridge will affect evangelism in the short term, and possibly the whole style and make-up of the church for many years to come.

I was privileged to be a member of the congregation at Holy Trinity, Brompton (HTB), an Anglican church in West London, at the start of the 1980s when it began an extraordinary period of growth. There was already much spiritual life, but I was not aware of many people becoming Christians. Then we held a mission based on small 'supper parties'. This was an ideal 'bridge' in that area, with many sociable young people in their twenties, and where most of the congregation were quite used to inviting friends for meals in their homes. Within two or three years the evening service had grown from 200 people to around 700 – and it has never stopped growing, with several church plants taking place, too.

Needless to say, more was happening at HTB than finding a culturally relevant means of evangelism, but I can still remember the change in the evening service after the mission. There always seemed to be new people 'popping in'. It was the bridge that allowed other forms of evangelism to operate – and it was easily repeatable in subsequent years. The 'S' curve was shooting sharply upwards!

In the next phase, particularly if the population with which you are in contact is 'receptive', and the new Christians have plenty of friends, growth can be rapid. This is because new Christians generally have many more non-Christian friends than those who have been members of the church for some years. At this stage evangelism ceases to be the problem. Instead the church has to work furiously to grow enough leaders to nurture the new Christians and manage a rapidly growing church.

Finally, and sadly, growth usually levels off as the church hits various constraints to growth. The building may be full, or there may be staff shortages. At this stage, also, evangelism is not the main problem, and much of the leadership's time is spent overcoming the constraints – maybe planning a building project, or possibly a church plant.

The precise nature of the growth dynamic, and the shape of the curve that describes it, will depend to a degree on the type of church and local community. The causes of eventual growth ceilings, for example, may be different in local community churches from eclectic ones. Nevertheless, the same principle must always apply: finding a culturally relevant means of evangelism is critically important at a particular stage in the growth curve – when the church is experiencing real spiritual life, but has not yet found a bridge into its local community or target population. I believe that is the position of many churches today.

2 The Road to Faith

In this chapter, and chapter 3, we consider some models to provide us with a language for talking about evangelism in part 2, the practical part of the book. In this chapter we look at the process of evangelism from the perspective of an individual moving towards faith.

Process and Crisis

Bishop Gavin Reid has said that 'Evangelism is a process rather than a crisis, though there may well be a crisis in the process.' I believe all Christian traditions are agreed on this, though the emphasis varies. Liberals place more stress on process. Evangelicals have traditionally placed importance on a crisis point of conversion, though they have rarely claimed it necessary for all. Catholics emphasize both process and crisis, locating the crisis in the liturgy.

In recent years, in Britain, there has been renewed emphasis on the process, or 'journey' of faith. This has come from several sources. From James Fowler and others who have investigated the way faith develops from a psychological perspective.[1] From recent research on how people become Christians, such as that already referred to carried out by Churches Together in England (which I shall call the 'CTE Research'). Above all, from the spiritual facts of life in our society, where the level of background knowledge of Christian faith is so much less than it was, with many young people unable even to say the Lord's Prayer. Evangelism, today, must start much further back. Across the board there has been a renewed emphasis on those forms of evangelization, such as enquirers' and catechumenate groups, which help people forward on their journey over a period of time.

Having said that, there frequently *will* be one or more points of crisis. Becoming a Christian is, after all, a massive step. It is stepping from spiritual darkness to light. It is an act of lifelong commitment. Whether the crisis point is baptism, or a baptism substitute such as an altar call, or simply a vital moment of decision which is remembered long afterwards, most of us value a moment to look back to. The CTE Research reported that 62% of adult converts described the process of coming to faith as gradual, and 38% as sudden.[2] Even for the gradualists, though, there will often have been key moments within the process.

Attitude or Belief?

Any secular marketing person knows that the 'crunch point' for whether strategies are effective lies in the minds of consumers. How will they make the decision to buy, and what will influence them? This will vary greatly for different products. Thus, a supplier of scientific equipment to industry knows that the decision to buy will be largely rational. A company selling beer or cigarettes, in contrast, knows that its customers will be influenced more by image and association of ideas than by detailed information. Advertisers therefore attempt to sway buyer attitudes rather than provide facts.

As evangelizers, we cannot get away from the fact that our aim is to influence people to 'buy' Christian faith. However lovingly, however respecting of a person's doubts and difficulties, at the end of the day we want them to become Christians! To devise a strategy, therefore, we need to understand how they will make that decision. Will it be on the basis of reason or attitude?

Both, surely, will be important, though the emphasis will vary from person to person, and at different stages in the journey. There are many roads to faith, but a high proportion of new converts would say that, early on, they were influenced by a Christian they knew. Something in that person's life fired them and challenged them. Without it they would have had no more interest in considering Christian faith than I, and probably you, have in the Jehovah's Witnesses. Later, of course, numerous intellectual difficulties may need to be faced, sometimes in considerable depth. It is amazing how the prospect of Christian commitment sharpens the mind!

Distance Models

If we acknowledge that some, at least, of the members of our community are involved in a journey towards faith, and, by implication, are at different distances from becoming Christians, it has important implications for evangelization. A preliminary question, though, is whether we need some means of expressing or evaluating the point they have reached in the journey.

Various measures are available. The best known is the Engel scale,[3] originally developed for radio evangelism overseas. On this scale, an individual or group who has no belief in the supernatural at all is classed as -10, whereas someone who feels the challenge of Christian commitment, for example, is rated at -2. The point of conversion is zero! Frankly, though I have no doubt the scale is invaluable for planning radio broadcasts, I cannot say I have ever been convinced of the benefit of trying to put numbers to people's distance from God in the local church context. If your sense of humour is suitably warped, though, it can be a source of mirth at church staff meetings!

Nevertheless, the *principle* of the Engel scale is important. It draws attention to the fact that evangelism is a process, as we have already discussed. People do not, usually, jump from −10 into Christian faith in one bound, and we have to face up to where people are 'at' when planning our evangelism. Guest services are of little use for '−10s'.

More useful still, conceptually, is a scale which differentiates between attitude and belief. The nearest I have come to this is the Sogaard scale,[4] used mainly for formulating missionary strategy. This measures both 'knowledge of Christ' and 'attitude to Christ' for different 'people groups'.

For the local church scene in the West I should like to adapt this slightly. I should like to replace 'knowledge' by 'belief', which will subsume at least some knowledge, and to broaden 'attitude' to include the Church as well as Christ and Christian teaching. In our society, many people have a positive attitude to Jesus Christ, or to what they know of him, but sadly they are put off by their image of the Church. Yet for almost everyone the Church is a major town on their road to faith.

Figure 2 uses this type of scale to show the position of two people. (A) is an intellectual who is quite cynical about Christian belief, but who has sung in church choirs in the past. There is no culture gap between him and the church, so he could rate high on the attitude scale. His problem is with belief. (B) is a working-class man from a council estate. Surveys have shown that levels of belief in God, and even belief that Jesus is the

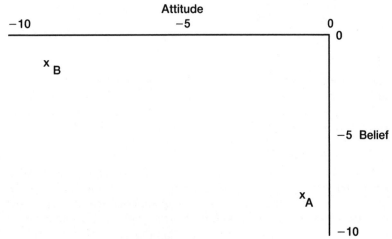

Figure 2   Attitude to and Belief in Christianity

Son of God, are higher on council estates than anywhere in Britain, yet
church attendance is lowest. Our man is representative. He apparently
has little problem with belief; for him the immediate barrier is attitude.
He views the church as 'wet', middle class, and mainly for women and
children. He would be embarrassed to be seen going there.

It will be seen at once that a negative attitude can be a kind of
'gatekeeper'. It may have arisen from various sources: from being forced
to attend boring services as a child, or from the image of the Church as
expressed by the media. I have known men who claim to have been
alienated by the snobbish attitude of a padre in the army. Whatever the
source, such blocks will need to be removed before the person is willing –
I am tempted to say *able* – to hear the gospel. Thus the journey to faith
may well look something like figure 3. The main movement, initially,
will be in attitude. As the journey proceeds there will be blocks which
hold back progress until they are broken through. There will be
setbacks. Ultimately, though, with much prayer and assistance, our
friend comes to a point when he or she can embrace Christian faith.

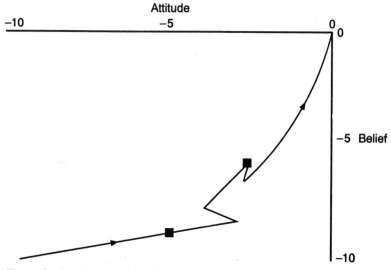

Figure 3   The Journey to Faith

The Three-Stranded Cord

How can we organize our evangelism, even the very life of our churches,
to assist this journey? Whatever we do, our influence will be limited.
The CTE Research made it clear that many of the events which help
people forward are simply the stuff of life: the death of a loved one; the
testimony of a neighbour enduring suffering; even an unsought mystical

experience. They cannot in any sense be managed. What we can do is to ensure that, when these events occur and someone is open to Christian faith, we are able to help them, not for just one step, but all the way to finding a strong and resilient faith.

It is far from easy in our culture for someone to come the whole way from complete disinterest to faith. Not only are there cultural and intellectual barriers. I, for one, am convinced that direct spiritual opposition can be very real.[5] The timing of unhelpful events can be extraordinary. You may have noticed the same thing.

It is all too easy for churches to help many people a little bit of the way, and then to leave them floating. I believe our programmes need built-in continuity, and I suggest that for this three elements are usually necessary:

- the Word of God (Christian teaching)

- the Friendship and personal witness of a Christian, preferably someone not too different from themselves (or the experience of Christian community)

- Prayer

In a different context, the book of Ecclesiastes speaks of the strength of a three-stranded cord.[6] I believe these three factors together have great strength to bring people to God. From now on I shall refer to them as the 'Three-Stranded Cord of Evangelism'.

I do not believe you will need much convincing of their importance. It is self-apparent that people will need teaching before they are able to respond intelligently to Christ. The Church initially grew as a result of the apostolic preaching.[7] Both Jesus and the prophets spoke of the spiritual potency of God's Word.[8] The Lausanne Congress may have been a little blinkered in *restricting* evangelism to proclamation, but few would deny that it is an essential part.

We can also see the impact of friendship and community. In the very early days of the Church it was the love and unity of the Christians which acted as a magnet to others, and historians agree that this remained an important element in the early Church's growth. There are also plenty of examples in Scripture of individuals bringing their friends and relatives to Jesus. The CTE Research reported that friends had been a significant influence for 61% of those finding faith.[9] They were most effective when they were examples of faith and normality,[10] and also for their support, love, and prayer.

Strangely, there is little in Scripture about intercession for the conversion of unbelievers, though there are plenty of examples of praying for power to witness. Nevertheless, Jesus prayed for his disciples, including Peter[11] when he could scarcely be considered a full believer. All evangelists are adamant as to the power and importance of prayer, wonderful stories abound, and most readers will need little convincing.

There is another element which some may feel I have omitted – the influence of 'signs and wonders' and healing ministry. We shall return to this in chapter 8. Sufficient to say, for now, that I recognize it and include it under Prayer in the Three-Stranded Cord.

What, then, is the practical relevance of the Three-Stranded Cord? Let me give one example which will be familiar to many readers. Two of the churches where I have served have had links with uniformed organizations, with young people, parents, and leaders attending regular parade services. I have always felt great warmth towards them, and have longed to help them find Christian faith but, along with many other ministers, I have had little success. Why? Let us consider the three strands of the Cord. Only one strand is in place. Those attending parades *do* hear the Word of God, but the Friendship and Prayer strands are usually missing, unless they happen to have a close friend in the congregation. One strand alone is insufficient to pull them all the way along the difficult journey to faith.

The Three Ps

A model for considering the journey of faith which will be familiar to some readers is the '3 Ps' of Presence, Proclamation and Persuasion.[12] Let us consider these categories and see how they relate to the Three-Stranded Cord.

'Presence' refers to Christian witness, primarily by deed, in a community. In the local church scene it could involve starting an advice centre or a mother and toddler group. It can also include the love and care shown by individual Christians, whether or not this is in the context of a church activity. In many cases such love will be accompanied by prayer. Thus Presence is equivalent to the Friendship strand of the evangelistic Cord, and often includes the Prayer strand as well.

'Proclamation' involves teaching or explaining the gospel message. This could include anything from a sermon to a Bible study course to a conversation over dinner. Thus it is really the same as the Word strand in the evangelistic Cord.

'Persuasion' is used in a very light sense. It is certainly not meant to imply any coercion. It refers to the process of discussion and questioning which takes place, particularly at the end of the faith journey, when someone is thinking seriously about becoming a Christian. It may include both church-run enquirers groups, and also informal late night cups of coffee! It therefore involves the Word strand in a more participative mode than previously, and often Prayer and Friendship, too.

I see little point in trying to be over-precise in the use of these terms. There is a degree of overlap between them, and naturally the journey of faith they are describing will vary from person to person anyway. Figure 4 gives a simplified version of how it might look for many people.

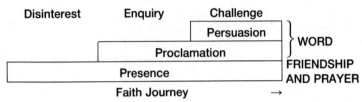

Figure 4   Relationship of the 3 Ps to the Three-Stranded Cord

Churches Together in England Research

Before closing this chapter on the journey to faith I should say a few words about the CTE Research,[13] to which I have already referred a number of times, and from which I will continue to draw extensively. It is probably the most important research on how people find faith ever carried out in Britain. It was a thorough piece of work, based on more than 500 questionnaires completed by people who had made a profession of faith as an adult. The respondents were chosen to give as representative a cross-section of English churches as possible.

The fact that it was based on individual responses, rather than assessments by ministers, has obvious advantages. It cut out a possible source of bias. Ministers, for example, might overestimate the effect of their sermons! They would also concentrate on the things that their own churches could influence. They might include the fact that someone was brought to church by a member of the congregation, but not the effect of an experience on holiday away from the church. The research method used avoided this bias.

The implications of the CTE Research being based on a roughly random sample also needs to be understood. It amounts to an advantage in reliability; though, arguably, a disadvantage in relevance. The question which was being answered was not 'What *could* be done?' but 'What *is* being done?' Actually, that overstates the point. John Finney interpreted the results with an eye to practical application. Nevertheless, the basic approach was geared to life in average churches, not to tracking down what was happening in exceptional churches.

My own more modest research project, on which this book is based, is different in three ways. First, it is church-oriented rather than individual-oriented. It looks, quite deliberately, only at those factors which a church can manage. Second, it tries to explore what *can* be done, rather than what is being done already. I have therefore sought out churches which are doing things extremely well, rather than trying to focus on the average church. Third, and as a consequence, its conclusions are of a more provisional nature. I nevertheless believe they are timely and significant. The project is described in chapter 4.

3 Growth Dynamics for Churches

In the last chapter we looked at the process of evangelism from the point of view of an individual enquirer moving towards Christian faith – from a micro perspective, if you like. We now need to develop a comparable conceptual framework at a macro level – from the perspective of a local church.

The Fringe

Few people would like to see themselves as 'fringe'. They might be insulted! Yet we all know that churches have a fringe, and they are vital for evangelism. A fringe is the fishing-pool. Without a fringe, evangelism is almost impossible. In terms of the distance models mentioned in chapter 2, most of those who are open to Christian faith and reasonably close to it will be in the fringe.

What exactly is the fringe? It is all those people who feel positive about their contact with the Church. It includes those who attend occasionally, such as at major festivals; those contacted through baptisms, weddings, and funerals; those who take the parish magazine; those who belong to church organizations or whose children attend the youth groups; and also those who are simply friends or relatives of church members.

The size and nature of the fringe can vary greatly. I have heard it suggested that the fringe is usually a third of the size of the congregation. That may have some basis in some areas, but it is certainly not universally true. An Anglican church in a leafy suburban area, or even more so in a country village where families have lived for generations, will probably have a large fringe. A free church in an inner city area or council estate may have no fringe at all, and will therefore find evangelism difficult. Geography plays a part, too. The North of England, Wales and Scotland are generally considered to have a greater deposit of 'folk religion' than the Midlands and South East, and this can reflect in higher attendance at Christmas, for example. There can be great variation, though, even between next door parishes. A church that has been the focus of a community in the past will have maintained a fringe if the population is stable, whereas a new church, or a church on an estate where most people only stay a few years, will not have had any opportunity of building such links.

How are we to think, clearly and constructively, about the fringe? Bishop Gavin Reid has suggested two categories which will be critical to our analysis:

- the *Institutional* fringe relate in some way to the church as an institution, that is to its organizations and services, and

- the *Personal* fringe are the personal friends and relatives of church members.

There can, of course, be an overlap. People can make friendships through church organizations, but I include these as Institutional fringe. I am limiting the definition of Personal fringe to relationships which exist anyway, apart from the church.

The Nature of Community

Self-contained, geographical communities do not exist today in the West in the way they did a hundred years ago. It may be sad, but it is a fact and we need to recognize it. The impact of the car, TV, and the telephone has meant that it is possible for many of the most significant relationships in our lives to be with people outside our immediate area. For better or worse, networks are the new communities of the West.

Many Anglicans, in particular, are blind to this. We speak of a community centre for example as being 'for all the community'. In reality, such centres only cater for a small percentage of certain groups. Now I do not want to quibble about language. Some sociologists define community in such a way that it must include a geographical dimension. For our purposes it will be better to recognize that the fragmented web relationships of modern society do supply at least some of the needs that were fulfilled by tighter geographical communities in the past. Like it or not, such imperfect community provides the context for our evangelism today.

Two Primary Models of Church

Since evangelism involves a social process, the type of evangelism which occurs will depend critically on the nature of a church's fringe, Personal or Institutional, and how the church interacts with that fringe. I believe that there are two primary models of how churches grow and draw in new members:

- the *Osmosis* model, which reaches its local geographical area through an Institutional fringe, and

- the *Web* model, which draws on a Personal fringe, and will usually reach out beyond its immediate area or parish.

Of course, there may be considerable overlap between these models, particularly in a tight community such as a village, or a traditional working-class area with many extended families. In such areas there will be a strong *local* network of personal relationships. Nevertheless, most of us can recognize the two different styles of church.

Very different styles of evangelization can be successful in Web and Osmosis churches, so it is vital for churches to understand their own growth dynamic.

THE OSMOSIS CHURCH

Under this model, there is a reluctance to count some people 'out' and others 'in'. The emphasis is on process rather than crisis. Many in the neighbourhood may view the church as 'theirs', and the priest or minister sees his job as drawing them towards the centre. The church is seen as a church for the area, rather than exclusively for its own congregation. In Britain the Osmosis church *par excellence* must be the Anglican or Church of Scotland village church, but I discovered from my research that many churches of all denominations see themselves as operating under this model, including Baptist and New Churches.

Such churches need to keep open boundaries. Attitudes need to be open too! Catholics and liberals are often better at this than evangelicals. Some evangelical congregations are so keen to get people converted, that they can appear confrontational and threatening. Such churches soon lose their fringe.

The Osmosis church has many strengths. It is the best model for providing 'salt and light' in a modest-sized local community. By taking the local area seriously, and not simply trying to 'save' individuals, it pays proper attention to Jesus' teaching on the kingdom of God. Sadly, though, I believe there are facets of modern British society which are making the Osmosis church less effective in many areas than it has been in the past. The Osmosis church needs two things: a sense of community, preferably with the church being at the centre of that community; and at least some nominal faith amongst the people it is trying to serve. Both these are declining in Britain.

THE WEB CHURCH

The Web church grows along natural relationship networks. Many new churches rely on webs, as they have no existing fringe. Sometimes they spiritualize this process. 'We just waited for those the Lord would send us.' By definition this means the friends of existing members! Web churches thrive best in car culture, where they can draw on a massive population. Well-known examples include city centre churches, often with many students and young professionals, and also ethnic churches. I had not realized that virtually all the black churches in this country, whom I had expected to be very locally based, are in fact Web churches drawing people from a distance. It is easy to see why. Kinship and friendship links are strong within any minority group, and it is just these links which make for a strong Web church.

Web churches can be extremely powerful in evangelism. Most of the largest British churches are Webs. The only exceptions I know of are some very large Roman Catholic churches, but these have not grown mainly by evangelism, but by attracting a large existing Roman Catholic population.

Nevertheless, Webs have some disadvantages. They have been criticized in the past, with some validity, as being proselytizers which do little to serve society. Those committed to a kingdom theology, and the notion of serving a parish, have found them hard to accept. Increasingly, though, the best Web churches are taking social action seriously, though it is sometimes city-wide rather than geared to the immediate locality. In many contexts the successful Web church can actually be off-putting to its local community. Village people can find it puzzling seeing the cars drawing up from far afield. They no longer feel it is 'their church'. They are suspicious. 'Lots of people come in cars from a long way away and give 'im lots of money. There's summat strange about that church.' A lass in her twenties was speaking about the 'other church' in the village.

There is another side to this coin, though. Osmosis churches, also, can exclude. Churches which supposedly cater 'for all the family' are not necessarily attractive to all groups, particularly to single people. I have often thought, as I walked round some local shopping centre, that it would be hard to imagine attracting many of the young people I saw there to most of our churches. Yet I could think of Web churches with many young people where there would be at least some possibility of them getting involved.

Homogeneous Groups

This leads us to a concept which has caused some strong feelings, for and against. The term 'homogeneous groups' was introduced by the late Donald McGavran, based on his observations of overseas mission work, mainly in India. McGavran noticed how most conversions to Christianity in India were as a result of 'people group movements'. In an area normally resistant to the gospel, sometimes one particular tribe would open up. Then large numbers of that tribe would become Christians. McGavran noted how such movements of the Spirit were often halted by the missionaries withdrawing the converts from their own culture into the missionary compound. This created a culture gap between the rest of the people and the new converts. McGavran came to believe that culture gaps were often a greater impediment to people becoming Christians than actual difficulties of belief. He noted that the best results came when missionary effort was concentrated on those tribes or other groups who had become open to the gospel, and such people were allowed to remain in their own culture. McGavran was a clear and analytical thinker who pushed ideas to their logical limits. He gives case after case, and is extremely persuasive. But most of his examples are from the developing world. Are his ideas valid in the West?

Even McGavran did not claim that all churches should operate on a homogeneous group basis. His overriding point was that there should be no unnecessary cultural barriers to people becoming Christians. In situations with very clear and distinct cultures he felt it vital to have monocultural churches, but he accepted that in 'social melting pots', such as the towns, where intermarriage and other mixing between tribes might be taking place, multicultural churches were possible and even desirable.[1]

Many people's objections to homogeneous groups are both predictable and understandable. The very concept appears to fall short of the New Testament vision of the Church where widely divergent cultures are 'all one in Christ Jesus'. I, for one, would find it completely unacceptable if churches were segregated on the basis of age, class, or race.

Nevertheless, I believe the case against homogeneous groups can be overstated. Let me say two things which I hope will add perspective to the debate. First, I have almost never heard, in Britain, of anyone setting out to build a homogeneous unit church. The only exceptions are some of the ethnic churches, which fulfil a specific need, and are always most welcoming when others visit; and the youth churches which, admittedly, are more controversial. They are few, I have not researched them, and I shall refrain from entering the debate.

What happens much more often is that a church, almost by accident, finds it is tapping into a receptive population, be it students, young professionals or some ethnic group. People start becoming Christians and inviting their friends, usually those from the same receptive group. Within a few years the church becomes a homogeneous unit church operating under a Web dynamic. Services change. Some of the previous, traditional members may leave. At no point has anyone planned it or read about Donald McGavran!

Second, we need to realize that Osmosis churches also use homogeneous groups. A mother and toddler group, or senior citizens' lunch club are obvious examples. I have never heard anyone object to these! Most of the times when I refer to homogeneous units in this book will be in the context of such groups operating within a more diverse church.

I have tried to rebut the caricature of McGavran's thinking which is sometimes presented, but, that done, I accept that readers will hold different viewpoints. These may well determine the attitudes taken to Web churches. In my opinion the benefits outweigh the objections. Web churches are providing an evangelistic cutting edge in today's society which most Osmosis churches lack. They are providing more than their fair share of converts and future ministers. They have a responsibility and need to understand their privileged role but, personally, I thank God for them.

Receptivity

Another term which I have already used, also developed by McGavran, is that of receptivity in a population. His observations over the years convinced him that, at certain times, particular 'people groups' became receptive or open to the gospel. Much of the rationale behind his theory of homogeneous groups was the need to make the most of such opportunities when they occurred, and to concentrate missionary effort where people were open and responsive.

How does this work in modern Britain? The concept of receptivity is more elusive than it may seem at first sight. Some of the most receptive groups can be those which, from the point of view of most churches, are very *unreceptive*. Groups such as young, single professionals in their twenties, or Nigerians who have recently arrived in Britain, may not be receptive as far as their local church is concerned; but, once in contact with the *right* church where they meet other people like themselves, they can become very receptive indeed. Such churches have known amazing growth in Britain in recent years. A possible illustration is a fire. Certain woods may have a high ignition temperature, but once ignited, will burn fast. This is the sense in which I shall be using the term 'receptive'. Once ignited, will the wood continue to burn? It will immediately be apparent that the sociability of the group is as important as the openness of individuals. Senior citizens may be quite open individually, but they are unlikely to invite large numbers of friends. Many students may be quite antagonistic to Christian faith, but Christian students should have a large enough circle of friends to find at least some who are open.

Further Models

This book is the result of a research project, the background to which is set out in the next chapter. At the start of the project I assumed that the growth dynamic of most churches would fall into one of two categories, Osmosis and Web, as just described. As a result of the research, however, a number of other models emerged. We shall leave some of them until chapter 13, but three of them need introducing now.

The Stepping-Stone church is a variation of the Web, enabling it to operate in a smaller and less receptive population. Like the Web, it draws on a Personal fringe, but rather than inviting contacts mainly to church services, an array of other events is organized. These may range from purely social occasions to evangelistic meals with a speaker. They take account of the fact that many, including the proverbial non-Christian husband, may have an attitude block as far as church services are concerned. Such folk will be more willing to come to events and, provided they meet Christians they can relate to and respect, they may well come to faith in gentle steps, whereas it would be too much to expect them to attend church in one jump.

The Open Door is a variation on the Osmosis model, and draws on the Institutional fringe. Whereas in the Osmosis church people find their way in through a variety of routes, in the Open Door there are one or two main ways in. These could be, for example, preparation for infant baptism or a particularly successful community group. Whereas, according to my findings, the Osmosis model can only work well where there is a reasonably strong sense of community, the Open Door can apply in a wider variety of contexts – provided the church can find such an open door.

A fifth model demands a mention. This is the Budding model, or cell group church. I did not discover it through my research. On the contrary, I was unable to find one British example of it operating successfully! We need to include it, though, because it is potentially the most powerful model of all. The biggest overseas churches are cell group churches, the most famous being the Full Gospel Central Church in Seoul, South Korea, with nearly a million members.

Under the Budding model, potential new Christians are not attracted either to services, or to community groups or special events. There is one main 'way in' and that is directly into 'cell' or home groups. These multiply, or 'bud' frequently to form new groups. The power of the method is that once the right cell group culture is created, growth continues with very little central intervention. There is no ceiling to growth. The very cells from which the church is constructed contain the power of multiplication and life.

I do not believe this model is operating in a complete sense in Britain at the moment, but there are churches using some of its principles with a degree of success. The potential is so enormous it deserves our consideration, and we shall look at it further in chapter 11.

Different Routes In

We conclude this chapter with figure 5 which summarizes the different routes in for the five models we have so far considered. It also shows how the various stages fit in with the 3 'Ps' of Presence, Proclamation and

Persuasion introduced in the last chapter. There are no strict rules. We shall come across many exceptions, but the diagram will serve as a plumb-line to alert us to interesting variations. It also sets out how the material is divided between the chapters in the next, more practical section of the book.

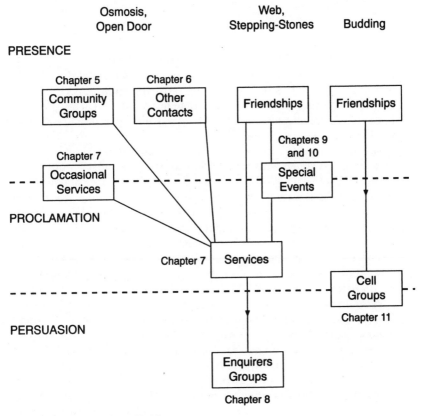

Figure 5   Routes to Faith

4 The Research Project

At this point, before we enter the main practical section of the book, it may be helpful if I explain the nature of the research project and my motivation in carrying it out. I shall include a few details of my own life, to enable the reader to understand 'where I'm coming from', and also the likely prejudices I bring to bear.

My first conscious experience of Christ as someone who is alive, and a force to be reckoned with in my life, was at a 'Crusader' youth camp when I was 11 years old. I had a classic evangelical conversion, and my twin brother and I returned home full of ardour, attempting to convert the vicar, the RE master and any other likely candidates we could find! I suppose my interest in evangelism goes back to that time. Even though I have never been a successful evangelist, it has always seemed the most important and valuable activity one could possibly be engaged in. Even now, nothing can thrill me more than somebody becoming a Christian.

After university I spent 14 years in business and industry before eventually persuading God that he should allow me into the ministry. During that time I spent 2 stimulating years at the Manchester Business School, which changed how I saw life. It became second nature to think strategically, to start from a 'top-down' perspective rather than from a 'worm's eye view', which is how most of my previous education had taught me to think. Much of this came through using the case-study method. For business after business we asked one question: 'What should this organization do next?' Some of my practical business experience reinforced this; for example, I worked in a strategic planning department, and also, just before I left for the ministry, as a management consultant. Asking the question, of course, is different from knowing the answer. Nevertheless, when faced with a business I thought I knew at least how to attack the problem. It was humbling when I later came to run a small church to discover that I had much less idea how to form such a strategy. If nothing else, my background had shown me what I didn't know!

While working in business, I was very involved in my spare time in various churches, mainly working with children and young people. Through most of that time, though, I never saw many adults become Christians. I suppose I did not really believe it happened. Most people became Christians as children or teenagers, and after that they were too caught up in 'the rat race' to make such a fundamental change. Then, in the 5 years before I went to theological college, I joined the congregation at Holy Trinity, Brompton. It was an extraordinary experience. The evening congregation grew from 100 to 700 in the 5 years I was there, and has kept on growing. I was influenced, personally, by the charismatic renewal, not in a dramatic way, but enough to make me feel more confident that I had something to give in ministry. I went to St John's, Nottingham, at the age of 35. St John's was an interesting and fulfilling time, though we did none of the top-down thinking which had characterized business school. We were never taught to run a church, or to think strategically. The syllabus, which of course was largely determined by the Church of England centrally, was of a traditional nature. I think all Bible colleges and theological colleges are the same. There was little emphasis on the case-study method.

I was not deterred by this. I valued learning the theology, and I believed I had seen enough at Holy Trinity, Brompton, to know how a church could grow. My first curacy was at Holy Trinity, Leicester, a city centre church, with many students and young people. It was not so different from HTB. It was less charismatic, and had a slightly different age and social mix, but the underlying dynamic was the same. It was a Web church.

The vicar, John Aldis, was very open to new ideas. In fact, they were not particularly new to him at all, as he had previously worked at All Souls, Langham Place. We organized 2 church missions, one of them with a considerable emphasis on small supper parties in people's homes, which I had seen work extremely well at HTB. We also started regular guest services with high-profile visiting preachers. It was quite successful. I suppose at most of the guest services around 10 young adults made some kind of response. They were encouraged to join nurture groups, and most of them grew well in the faith. I was reasonably confident that I knew how a church should tackle evangelism, and the only thing that puzzled me was why more churches didn't do the same!

My next move was to a daughter church in Birmingham, St Stephen's Church Centre, part of the parish of St Stephen and St Wulstan's, Selly Park. The Church Centre was an 'ordinary' family congregation, meeting in a hall. The worship was informal, which I liked, and there was a wonderful sense of mutual support and fellowship. Nevertheless, it was completely different from Holy Trinity, Leicester, and I wondered if my approach to evangelism would work. I soon realized that things were going to be very different, and certainly the guest services were not usually a success. Even so, in my first year, to my astonishment, around 20 people became Christians. It was usually completely unpredictable. Some of them had the kind of stories you read in 'those books'! I still do not understand quite how it happened, and I can only put it down to God's graciousness. After the first year though, when we were 'flying high' as a fellowship, things seemed to dry up. I realized that there was no repeatable pattern as there had been at Leicester. We were a local area church, but few of our members had friends or family living locally whom they could easily invite to our services or activities. We simply did not have a 'way in' to the local community, which, anyway, was very fragmented. The Church Centre, together with the larger parish, was a marvellous place to be part of, but I was deeply frustrated at not knowing the way forward in evangelism. Books did not seem to help in the least. They always seemed to promote some ideal method which had worked in some place which was culturally quite different from the church and area I was part of. Slowly the idea and determination developed inside me to carry out some research, and possibly to write a book, looking at how a church should develop a viable evangelistic strategy, taking account of local culture.

To avoid misunderstanding, perhaps I should make clear the meaning I attach to the word 'research'. I am anxious not to invest my findings with a false sense of objectivity by my use of the word – and I cannot think of an alternative. Its everyday usage varies from the very informal, for example researching a TV programme or even a holiday, to the very formal, as in a carefully controlled scientific project. I use the word quite broadly. The research reported on here has varied from the very informal, which could be compared to investigative journalism, to the slightly formal, mainly analysis of limited sample surveys. At each point I shall do my best to explain the basis and degree of objectivity of my findings.

To enable me to carry out the research I obtained a third curacy, working part-time, at St Mary of Bethany Church in Woking. I was able to give 2 days a week to the research project, which lasted just over 2 years. All the research, and most of the writing of this book, took place during this period, and I am very grateful to St Mary's for their support. As I write the final touches I have just started as vicar of another St Mary's, in Greenham near Newbury. No doubt they will have to suffer me trying out some of the ideas in practice!

Quite early on I arrived at an overall philosophy:

1. The research had to be practical, and relate to ordinary British churches. I did not want to write about what worked in mega churches overseas.

2. I had to limit it to adult evangelism. It was not that children and youth were unimportant, but they were a massive area of study in their own right, and my own experience in recent years had been mainly with adults.

3. I had no illusion about inventing something new. I was only too

aware that the greatest ideas can hit problems in practice. I knew that many exciting things were already happening in British churches and my task was to report on what the Holy Spirit was already doing, and how this varied in different cultures.

Thus much of the research was to consist of interviews with ministers at the cutting edge. I believed that the choosing of hypotheses to test would be as important as the testing. Thus much of the first year was deliberately spent 'networking', trawling around on the phone, pestering busy ministers and trying to find useful leads as to new ideas which were working in particular cultures or church situations. In total I carried out 130 interviews, with 30 personal visits and 100 lengthy conversations on the telephone. Insights from many of these are included as case studies in the next section of the book.

Initially I was expecting the structure of the findings, and therefore of the book, to relate primarily to culture. I expected to have chapters on the inner city, rural areas, city centre parishes, etc. I moved from this approach for two reasons. I discovered that the sheer subtlety and diversity of the different cultures was far greater than I had imagined. Two different council estates, or different villages, could be the homes of vastly different social dynamics. More and more I discovered that the style of evangelism necessary depended more on the pattern of relationships existing in the community, and between the church and the community, than on culture per se.

By the end of the first year I was able to start focusing the research. I therefore designed a survey for sending out to churches (see appendix 1). I had a problem. The first survey was quite complex and I was not sure if ministers would be willing to complete it. In particular it asked for an analysis of the ways in which people had become Christians in the last 5 years, and I doubted if most clergy would have this kind of information available. In the end, I decided that if anyone would know, it would be my fellow members of the British Church Growth Association! The church growth movement is committed to careful research and I felt at least some of the ministers would be able to complete the forms. I was pleasantly surprised with 48 forms being returned, amounting to a 40% response rate. Not surprisingly, some ministers could not complete the analysis of ways in which people were first contacted (question 10) and the evangelism factors (question 11). This applied particularly to priests or ministers responsible for Osmosis-style churches, where a host of different factors influence someone's way into the fellowship.

The most important finding from the first questionnaire was the existence of the Stepping-Stones and Open Door models in addition to the Osmosis and Web models I had started with. I now needed to test the existence of these models beyond the mainly evangelical membership of the BCGA. I therefore designed a second, somewhat simpler survey and sent it to 160 churches, 70% of which were of catholic or liberal churchmanship. This was done through the agency of the Christian Research Association, based on their records from the English Church Census. The churches were intended to be 'growing churches' with attendance between 100 and 200, and the responses mostly fitted these criteria. Once again, there was an encouraging response rate of 41%.

Thus the research involved 2 main questionnaires and also a large number of interviews, mainly on the telephone. It also included modest studies of parent and toddler groups, men's groups, and Proclamation evangelism. Details of these are included in the relevant sections of the book.

I have tried to cover a broad spread of British churches. I deliberately left out Northern Ireland as, with 70% church attendance in that country, I believed the dynamics of evangelism would be quite different. I have to admit considerable, though unintended, bias towards England, partly because of my own range of contacts and, in the case of the second survey, as a result of the churches being derived from the English Church Census.

The reader will have noticed that the combined sample size of the surveys, 114 forms being returned in all, was not large. This will need to be taken into account in interpreting the results. The surveys were not intended to be a representative sample of all British churches. They will be used with caution to give insight into the general picture of church life, but their main purpose was to give leads to interesting churches and patterns of ministry for further investigation.

An analysis of the results of the 2 surveys is contained in appendix 2. Further discussion is included in the relevant chapters in the main text.

PART 2
The Tactics –
Getting to Grips

In this section of the book we consider the 'nuts and bolts' of evangelism as a prelude to looking at strategy formulation in part 3. The reader may find it helpful to refer from time to time to the diagram on p. 25 to regain a sense of overall perspective.

We start the section by considering ways of creating and evangelizing an Institutional fringe, beginning with community groups in chapter 5. We look at other ways of attracting such a fringe in chapter 6, with the exception of contacts through the 'occasional offices' of weddings, baptisms, and funerals which we consider in the context of church services, in chapter 7. Chapters 8 and 9 deal with Persuasion and Proclamation evangelism, and chapters 10 and 11 look at the specific issues of reaching men and of motivating the congregation.

5 Community Presence – Groups

By community groups I mean groups, usually of a social nature, where 'the church meets the world'. Members may include personal friends of church people, though more often they are folk from the local community, drawn in by advertising or pastoral contacts. They are more often Institutional fringe than Personal fringe.

The groups need not be run by the church, though we shall mainly be considering ones which are. The prime purpose need not be evangelism. In some cases, such as a church-run job club or nursing home, the aim would probably be almost entirely social action. I am not suggesting the aim of any group *should* be evangelism, but where the church has decided that evangelism is to be one of the aims, we need to consider how it can be achieved.

The research survey had a question about community groups (see appendix 2, table A3). Three types of group were listed: parent and toddler groups; groups for senior citizens, which obviously included most lunch clubs; and men's groups. In addition churches were invited to list other groups. These included a huge range: sports activities such as dance classes, keep fit, bowls, badminton and football; groups to meet social needs including the unemployed and homeless; cafés and drop-in centres; and day or evening classes, usually appealing to women, for flower arranging, sewing, etc. In addition there was a wide variety of clubs and activities for children and youth, though, as we have seen, these were not included in the research.

By far the most frequently occurring groups were parent and toddler and senior citizens' groups, followed by men's groups. The only other type of group reported with sufficient regularity to include in the analysis was a variety of other women's groups. These ranged from meetings with a speaker to informal coffee mornings. They included groups which were purely social, and others with some spiritual content. Out of 119 churches, the number with groups was as shown in table 1.

It may be that the number of women's groups is understated, since it was not a preselected category on the survey form. It will be seen that most groups, regardless of churchmanship, included evangelism as an aim.

The research approach taken was to concentrate on the most frequent

	Number of Groups	Aim Includes Evangelism
Parent and Toddler	74	94%
Senior Citizens	59	95%
Men's Groups	27	79%
Women's Groups	17	93%

Table 1   Church Groups

type of group – parent and toddlers – to try to assess what were the factors which led to effective evangelism. We therefore consider parent and toddler groups first, and then look briefly at other kinds of group to see whether the conclusions might apply more widely.

I also carried out a small study of men's groups. Most of these, however, did not really turn out to be community groups in the sense of a social or Presence evangelism activity. Many are centred on Proclamation events and enquirers' groups. We therefore consider men's evangelism separately in chapter 10.

Parent and Toddler Groups

I spent 5 baffled years wondering how we could evangelize our mother and toddler group in Birmingham. I was confident it was the best group in the area. That is why we always had a waiting list. We had a large hall, with around 25 mums, as well as the occasional dad and grandma, and about 35 babies and toddlers per session. We had good toys and equipment, and, more important, loving and committed Christian leadership. A small group prayed regularly. To our great joy, 2 or 3 of the women became Christians and joined the church. Yet they were the exceptions. It was rare that we had visitors from the group on Sunday, even for our Mothering Sunday service.

What was wrong? I thought I had one or two of the answers. The group was too big. With only, sometimes, 4 or 5 Christians attending, they were too few to influence the overall atmosphere. Also, there was a culture gap between the mums, most of whom would have described themselves as working class, and the church. Not that we were a strongly middle-class church. Our members came from a mix of backgrounds and we tried hard to use ordinary language. Yet the idea of coming to church on a Sunday morning was a distinct turn-off to many of our mums, and even more so to the dads. I concluded that most parent and toddler groups which were having success in evangelism were probably in plush, middle-class areas, or places where church-going was more normal.

Still, I was determined to try. At my suggestion, the leaders introduced a time of chorus singing, and sometimes a story. It was entirely voluntary, but most of the mums, with their children, attended. It was a success as far as it went. The children enjoyed the choruses and used to sing them at home. The mums approved, but no one came to church.

We decided to be more ambitious. From time to time I would show a few minutes of a Christian testimony video. I used to wheel my TV over in a barrow, and I must have looked a strange sight! On one occasion a much loved member of the group told his own story of how Jesus Christ had changed his life. It was not that anyone was against us. They always responded with warmth. But somehow, there was a gap, and we did not know how to close it. I remember walking back from the hall in the rain, my TV set in my barrow, feeling distinctly dejected. 'What is the point?' I thought, 'We are not getting anywhere.' I resolved at that time to find out how effective evangelism could work in a group such as ours, if I possibly could.

PARENT AND TODDLER SURVEY

How successful are parent and toddler groups generally? The survey asked churches to estimate the effectiveness of different groups in drawing outsiders into the Church. The results in percentage terms for those groups which included evangelism as an aim were as shown in table 2.

Effectiveness in Evangelism	%
None	7%
Little	33%
Adequate	30%
Good	30%

Table 2   Evangelistic Effectiveness of Parent and Toddler Groups

It may seem encouraging that 60% of the churches regarded the effectiveness of their groups as adequate or good, but I believe that would be optimistic. Of the churches covered by my first survey, which also gave details of how people had become Christians, 9 rated their groups in the 'good' category. Of these, however, only 3 appeared to have even one person a year becoming a Christian through their parent and toddler group. In my opinion, having had conversations with a number of the ministers involved, it is probable that less than 10% of the groups overall were having even one person a year becoming a Christian through their efforts.

Yet I *have* come across groups which are extremely effective. What is their secret?

THE APPROACH

It needs to be said that I have not encountered any kind of community group, toddler groups included, which yields an avalanche of converts – not in Britain. We shall find nothing to compare with the large Web churches, for example. Nevertheless, I have found several churches where an average of 3 to 5 women are becoming Christians each year through parent and toddler groups.

I have found these groups on the 'grapevine'. Several of the best leads came through the Families and Under Fives Ministry of the Church Pastoral Aid Society. Partly for this reason, most of them are Anglican and evangelical. I do not claim they form a representative sample.

I have used what researchers call, euphemistically, an inductive approach. I cannot claim my findings are more than tentative conclusions for further study. At the very least, there may be cultures or church situations where they do not all apply. They are based on lengthy conversations with 15 leaders of successful parent and toddler groups. Let us first look at 2 of these groups.

☐   St George's, Ovenden, Halifax, is an Anglican church serving a mixed area with both middle-class and Urban Priority Area (UPA) council house areas in the parish. Mothers from both backgrounds are involved in the parent and toddler work. There are 2 toddler groups, with around 30 mums in each, meeting on Monday and Wednesday mornings for 2 hours. The aim of both groups is simply to provide the best mother and toddler provision possible. There is nothing specifically Christian in the group sessions, though team members talk actively about their faith in an informal way. Anne Croft, the church's Families and Under Fives Coordinator, leads both groups.

Each toddler group is run by a team of 5 women, most of whom have become Christians through the group. There is an emphasis on both prayer and training. The women's Bible study group, 'Power Point', consists mainly of the toddler group team, and its members are all involved in prayer triplets. The group also provides training. For example, it has used the video course *Person to Person* for training in personal evangelism. Thus, all the team members are able to share their faith with the other mums.

In addition to the help received through Power Point, there is a monthly team prayer meeting, and the group makes use of the local 6-week Pre-School Playgroups Association training programme. Two of the women are trained to use a shortened 3-week version of the home-based enquirers' course Good News Down the Street (see p. 81).

. Enquirers' groups are held at different times. Some women join the 15-week 'Christians for Life' course organized by the church in the evenings. Daytime enquirers' groups are also held, on Thursday or Friday mornings when the playgroup serves as an effective crèche.

The group arranges special events with guest speakers from time to time, and also a termly 'Open House' evening to which husbands are also invited. At least 20 mums have become Christians through the group in the last 5 years.

☐ St Paul with St Stephen, Hyson Green, is an Anglican church in a multiracial UPA area, with many single mums. June Kirkham is a full-time volunteer worker, and is responsible for the women's activities and also baptism preparation under the direction of the curate.

The women's work is extensive, with a playgroup for 2½ hours every weekday morning, in addition to the parent and toddler group. The latter is held on Thursday and Friday, and lasts from 9 a.m. to 3.30 p.m., with between 15 and 30 adults present at any time. There is no formal team. Planning and prayer sessions are open to all, and the more committed folk come, including some non-Christians.

The group seeks to have a clearly Christian ethos. All literature makes clear that it is a Christian group 'seeking to put faith into action'. The day begins with a Bible study to which anyone can come, and which takes place in the hall where the group meets. Those who do not wish to take part sometimes listen in, and give requests for prayer. Mums are encouraged to leave their children with the playgroup, particularly during this time, which helps meaningful conversations develop.

In addition to the Bible study during the group, there are various opportunities for the mums to discover more about Christian faith. The women's Bible study group, which is held on a Monday lunch-time, involves several who are not yet Christians. There is an open 'any questions' approach. Some simply come to listen in. Also, from time to time, a Christian 'basics' group is run using the Study by Extension for All Nations (SEAN) Abundant Life course. Not all the women who take part are literate, so June or one of the other women visit them at home to help them complete the worksheets which form part of this course. The course is run in such a way as to relate it to the questions which children ask, and many of the women find this helpful.

Once a term there is an evangelistic service including the children. As many of the playgroup children as possible are involved, for example by dressing them up in various ways. Even the Asian mums from other faith backgrounds are happy to come. Sometimes there is a talk by the vicar or June, though the testimony of a mum they know well is usually the most effective. It needs to be said that there is much hubbub in these 30-minute services!

The group has a lively social programme with days out and a family camp in the summer. At Christmas there is a disco to which partners come, with an evangelistic speaker.

Over the last 5 years at least 20 women have come to faith. Most now come to church, though for some the Bible study is their church. About 10 husbands have also become Christians over the 5 years.

As a result of the interviews I have arrived at 7 'keys' for structuring a parent and toddler group for effective evangelism. I need to stress that these are not all that is needed. Some may say I have missed out the most vital things, such as love and openness, and efficient organization, and above all, prayer. The fact is, others are much better qualified to write on the day-to-day running of a group than I am. Excellent books are available.[1] This book is solely concerned with *strategy*. I am writing as much for ministers as for parent and toddler group leaders.

Before we turn to the 7 'keys', may I try to answer a possible objection. Is it not true that the success of a group will depend critically on factors external to the running of the group itself – such as being part of a very lively church, and having an exceptionally gifted toddler group leader? If so, does it mean that other groups cannot replicate their success?

I accept there is some validity in this. Of course, the number of people becoming Christians will depend on the church, area, and available leadership. The 2 cases above are very successful groups which have developed over a number of years. Nevertheless I believe that the principles below are valid. They will help most groups to be more effective. What is more, although many of the leaders I have spoken to have been gifted by God in evangelism, they would deny being exceptional. Most would say they have learnt by doing, and trying to be open to God. The 'keys' amount to no more than providing a channel through which the Holy Spirit can flow.

SEVEN 'KEYS'

Key 1   There Must Be an Agreed Evangelistic Aim

There is nothing surprising about this. Evangelism in the chaotic atmosphere of a toddler group is far from easy. What is more, the team will change frequently, as their own children grow older or they get other jobs themselves. Unless evangelism is clearly agreed as one of the aims by the minister as well as the parent and toddler group leaders, any evangelistic vision will fade. Nothing will happen.

Key 2   A Trained and Committed Team

I used to think that a parent and toddler club was a natural place for Christians to share their faith. All the mums who had a relationship with Christ ought naturally to share that with the others. I deluded myself! The reality is that most of the Christian mums are going for what they can get out of it. They have little energy to convert anyone! The people who will build relationships and help people to become Christians are the members of the team.

It is not enough to have an informal group who help out. It must be a clear and recognized team. I concede that the Hyson Green group does not have a formal team, but this is the exception. Most groups, particularly where there is no specifically Christian input, found the need for a formal team to start building relationships and talking about Christian faith.

It is vital, therefore, that the team members are trained, and built up, and encouraged. There will need to be prayer and planning meetings, and everyone will need a role. The value of training in giving confidence should also not be underestimated.

Some groups use the secular training provided by the Pre-School Playgroups Association. CPAS organize excellent training days.[2] Several leaders said I should 'plug' these! There are also a number of resources and training courses available for training in personal evangelism. We look at Evangelism Explosion in chapter 8. I have been in churches where the wrong people attend courses in personal evangelism. Serious minded folk with no non-Christian friends turn up, but the people who are really at the interface, such as the leaders of the community groups, are the ones who should really be there.

Key 3   The Group Should Not Be Too Big

I have already mentioned how, when I was in Birmingham, I had a suspicion that a large group might make evangelism more difficult. Several leaders have confirmed this. Groups have their own dynamic, and the larger the group, the more likely people are to split up into small groups or cliques, and the harder it is to build relationships. One leader felt that 15 mums was the maximum, before the noise level became distracting and cliques developed. Another put the limit at 25. I am not saying that there are no successful groups with more than this, but the larger the group, the greater the skill in building relationships that is demanded of the team; and relationships are the stuff of evangelism.

I have come across one or two groups which actually met in homes. On one tough council estate the women from the main toddler group met informally in what were effectively mini toddler groups in homes, one group for each tower block. It met an important social need, but the value for evangelism will also be apparent. In cases like this, 'Small is beautiful'.

If evangelism is the aim, the best advice to someone starting a parent and toddler group from scratch, from what I have seen, would be to start small.

Key 4   The Need For Small Group Evangelism

A question we shall face frequently is assessing which of several options is the most helpful route for coming to faith. We know from the CTE Research that for many people the first step is starting to come to church. Is this the case for a toddler group mum?

At one stage I believed the most effective way in would be through a pram service. I knew that many mums were happy to come to these and it seemed a small jump from this to a low key, relaxed, all-age service. I had certainly read and heard enthusiastic reports of pram services and their potential for evangelism.

I can only say that I have not discovered any church where this approach yields significant evangelistic results. I am not wanting to knock pram services. They can be valuable in starting to raise questions of faith in those who attend. Nevertheless, the jump from a mid-week pram service to a Sunday morning service is usually too great. It does sometimes happen, particularly where there is a weekly family service or where the parents are enquiring about infant baptism. Generally, though, amongst the churches I have investigated, it does not work.

The toddler groups in which most people were becoming Christians all used some kind of small group evangelism. Usually this was an enquirers' or 'basics' group, some using either a video or Bible study material, others an 'any questions' approach. It was important to make the jump from toddler group to the small group as easy as possible. The enquirers' group usually had to be on a separate day from the main toddler group session, but it had the ethos of 'something we go to'. At Judith Wigley's group in Pudsey near Bradford, the mums could be heard saying to each other 'See you on Friday'. 'What's Friday?' would be the reply. Interest had been aroused. The group must not seem like some strange church activity, but something *we* do, the people I have got to know and trust.

Some groups also use Good News Down the Street. This is a 7-week enquirers' course carried out in the person's own home. We explain it in more detail in chapter 8. When Jill Murphy was at St James, Birkenhead, an Anglican church in a very deprived area, her husband, Roger, a Church Army captain, used to follow up and visit toddler group members and parents of baptized children in their homes and, where possible, did the course with couples. It was extremely successful. Over 3 years there, 40 people were converted through *Good News Down the Street*, and for at least 12, the parent and toddler group was the contact. The great advantage of this approach was that it pulled in the dads! It has to be said, though, that Roger is gifted as an evangelist with men.

Key 5   Integrated Leadership

We have seen that the most natural route to faith for someone attending a toddler group is through an enquirers' group. In that case, it is vital that mums find it as easy as possible to join such a group. The group needs to be at a convenient time and must be 'owned' by the toddler group members. The easiest way to ensure this cooperation is by having the enquirers' group and parent and toddler club under joint leadership.

The same can be said of the young women's Bible study groups, and of any baptism preparation teams. I am not wanting to be dogmatic. Every church is different. There must be, though, a high degree of coordination, and one way to achieve it is integrated leadership.

Key 6 Specifically Christian Input

I am 'sticking my neck out' on this one and I have deliberately left it till almost last. Should a toddler group have some specifically Christian input? Clearly, it is possible to argue both ways. Hyson Green and Ovenden are examples of groups which have taken alternative points of view.

In my opinion, either approach can work, but the totally open approach is a harder one to make work evangelistically, and needs more skilled leadership. Some formal Christian input puts Jesus and church onto the agenda. Some kind of singing and story time for the children, rather like a mini pram service, is one way of doing this. Even more valuable, in my view, is an approach like the open Bible study at Hyson Green, which made it clear that Christian faith is about real issues in our everyday adult lives. Some groups organize an occasional speaker on a range of topics from cooking to health to the Bible. Clearly, you need a crèche for this. One way or another, though, particularly for a new group, it seems common sense that some kind of Christian input will help 'break the ice'.

I heard of one small toddler group where all the mums who asked to come were told it would be a specifically Christian group, though there would be a crèche throughout. None objected, the crèche was everything! Within a very few weeks, on alternate weeks, the whole group was studying the video series *Jesus Then and Now*. Admittedly these were middle-class mums, and perhaps that example is at one end of a spectrum. Nevertheless, it illustrates how a smaller group with specifically Christian aims can start to look at spiritual issues, even with only one or two trained leaders. Let the reader decide.

Key 7 Halfway Houses and Special Events

I am leaving this key till last, because neither halfway houses nor special events are essential steps in the evangelization process. Nevertheless, they are valuable catalysts, particularly for new groups where starting an enquirers' group may prove quite hard in the early days.

Let me mention two types of halfway house. One is a Christian parenting group. These have been held, with some success over the years, at St Mary of Bethany Church in Woking. One advantage is that people will come as couples, and I know of several dads who have attended a Christian 'basics' group and become Christians, as a result of first attending a parenting course. Similar, but with a slightly different emphasis, are groups on how to talk to our children about God.

Special events can have a similar impact. I am talking about both purely social events, and those with some kind of Christian speaker. Once again, I have a suspicion that these may be particularly important for a group needing to experience 'lift off'. I know of one group where several women became Christians following a coffee morning with a guest speaker. One important question is whether these should be evening events, to which husbands are invited, or daytime events geared mainly to the mums. My suggestion is that the former are preferable, but that it would be wise to start with the latter, unless you are aiming mainly at the husbands of wives who are already Christians. It is trying to jump over two hurdles in one go to expect a non-Christian mum to drag her non-Christian husband to some evangelistic event! A beer and skittles evening would be another matter.

Other Groups

To what extent can our conclusions for parent and toddler groups be applied to other kinds of church-run groups? Is it possible that there may be principles which apply to most kinds of group? In this section we shall not be drawing on further research, but considering some suggestions, which might merit further study, arrived at by reflecting on the toddler group study and some other case material.

First, let us consider the relative effectiveness of the 3 most popular types of group. Table 3 summarizes the ministers' estimates of the evangelistic impact of those groups which included evangelism as an aim. It will be seen that, if anything, the parent and toddler groups are the most effective. Yet we have seen that this does not mean a great deal.

| | | Evangelistic Impact | | |
	None	Little	Adequate	Good
Parent and Toddler	7%	33%	30%	30%
Senior Citizens	11%	22%	45%	22%
Men's Groups	9%	36%	32%	23%

Table 3   Evangelistic Impact of Church Groups

Table 4 considers the average number of new Christians per year from each type of group. This table is only in respect of the first survey, as it was only those forms which gave the contact sources for new Christians. It will be seen that none of the types of group yielded an average of more than 0.3 new Christians per year. I think it is reasonable to conclude that most of the groups are not very effective.

	Number of Groups	New Christians over 5 Years	Average New Christians per Year
Parent and Toddler	29	49	0.3
Senior Citizens	27	15	0.1
Men's Groups	15	21	0.3

Table 4   New Christians from Church Groups

THE SEVEN 'KEYS' AND OTHER GROUPS

Let us now consider whether any of our proposed keys for effective evangelization for parent and toddler groups may apply more widely to other types of church-run community groups.

Key 1   An Agreed Evangelistic Aim

Exactly the same thinking applies for other groups as for parent and toddler groups. Evangelism is hard. Unless the aim is clear, any group will lose its evangelistic edge. We shall see how this has happened to some men's groups in chapter 10. None of the strategies below, such as team training in evangelism and provision of an enquirers' group, will happen unless the aim is clear.

Key 2   A Trained and Committed Team

The desirability of a trained and committed team is almost self-evident, but its practicality will depend on the kind of group. It would not be realistic to expect leaders of some groups to have formal training. Let us say that a group of women decide to get together for an hour after work once a week to run an aerobics class, with the aim of drawing in outsiders. How would they be trained, and would they be willing to receive it? Either way, it would be vital for the core group to get together regularly to pray for the venture. Without that, any evangelistic drive would fade out.

It is difficult to be dogmatic. Groups are so different from each other. All we can say is that, where possible, there should be a definite team. In many cases training, preferably in evangelism, will be valuable.

Key 3   Size

Once again, the variety of groups is so great that it is hard to be dogmatic. Nevertheless, one can see that the reasons which made a small group desirable with parents and toddlers will apply to many other groups. Let me give an example from youth work.

The Romsey Mill is a Christian youth project operating in Cambridge. Some years ago, a previous leader, Mike Breen, and his team decided to close the youth club. This large group had not provided very helpful dynamics for evangelism. The youth leaders found their main role was that of policemen, controlling the group and protecting the buildings! Also there were unhelpful cliques, with an older group of boys dominating the rest. Instead, it was decided to start a series of small groups which Mike Breen now calls 'A Teams'. Each 'A Team' had 2 leaders who helped a small group of young people plan a programme for a 6-week period, and then joined with them in putting it into effect. The approach was very popular with the young people, and drew 3 times as many as the original youth club. More important, it built up much better relationships between the leaders and the young people. Many became Christians as a result.[3]

One can see the same principle operating in youth camps and holiday missions. Without small groups there would be chaos. Is there any reason why the same principle should not apply to adults? Small groups help relationships to develop, thus allowing the Three-Stranded Cord to operate. May I make a commonsensical proposition? In Presence evangelism activities the size of the overall group should either be kept manageable, or else it should be divided into small groups.

Keys 4, 5, and 7   Appropriate Link Strategies
I use the phrase 'link strategies' to refer to the underlying principle behind the use of enquirers' groups and also specific events and halfway houses. We are talking '3 P' evangelism. The need is to move people on from the Presence activity to the most helpful next stage in their faith journey. The question is, 'What is the most helpful next step?' We have seen that, for a toddler group, it is usually an enquirers' group, but this will not be so for all groups. In the case of a men's football team, for example, most men would not be too quick to join an enquirers' group, but might come first to a dinner with a well-known sportsman as the speaker.

For a senior citizens' group there may be more than one viable approach. Many retired people have at least some Christian background from their youth, and there is no great culture gap to prevent them attending a church service at an appropriate time of day. Equally, several churches I have been involved with have run daytime home groups for older people, and these have been extremely helpful. For senior citizens we are usually talking about a warming-up of latent faith rather than a clear conversion, though the latter does happen occasionally.

For youth, it has been accepted for some time that the usual way in is through a youth group. Only in the youth congregations do young people join a church service first, in any numbers. In both the youth group and the youth service, of course, the homogeneous unit principle is at work. Even though we are not considering young people's evangelism in any detail, I should like to give another case study of some youth work as it is such an excellent example of a church putting together some viable link strategies.

☐ The Lantern Church, Canford Magna, is a strongly charismatic evangelical Anglican church a few miles north of Bournemouth. David White, the vicar when I researched the case, had arranged with Youth With a Mission (YWAM) that they would base one of their discipleship training schools, which is attended by about 10 people from around Britain, at the church. With the help of these folk, the church runs an effective youth work which draws young people in through 4 different stages.

The first stage, through which initial contact is made, is a series of Rave Clubs which are advertised widely. There is loud music, but no drugs!

The next stage are 'Night Bins'. These are smaller than the Raves. Once again there is some loud music, but there is also a gospel talk, and there is prayer for healing. Many of the young people have difficulties with drugs and other problems, and this prayer is much appreciated. There is active personal work by the team, many of whom use spiritual gifts in a powerful way, sometimes having insights into young people's lives specifically revealed by God. Many have become Christians through this and go on to the next stage.

The third stage is the cell groups which are held on a Sunday afternoon. These are mainly for those who have made a commitment to follow Christ, and those who come are committed also to attending the evening service, which is the fourth stage. When I visited the church, the youth work had only been in operation for 2 years, but there were 130 young people aged between 15 and 25 at the evening service.

I have said nothing so far about key 5, integration of leadership. It is difficult to generalize, but the general rule must be that, the greater the culture gap between those in the community group and the church, the more important it will be that the enquirers' group or Bible study is led by people they already know and relate to. The last case study is a good example of this. The unchurched young people would never have attended the cell groups if they were not run by the youth leaders they already knew and respected.

Thus, carefully planned link strategies are likely to be important for all types of church-run community groups. Some form of enquirers' group or other small group will frequently be important, though it may not be the first stage.

Key 6: Specifically Christian Input

Some kind of Christian input will clearly be more appropriate in some kinds of group than others. Clearly, it would not be feasible in a sports club, though occasional special events might still be very acceptable. Nevertheless, as with the toddler groups, I believe the principle stands that some Christian input will usually serve as a useful conversation starter, if nothing else. It may be a regular short spot. It may be a once-a-term special activity. We need to be alive to the opportunities. At St Cuthbert's, Fulwood in Preston, they use a 'basics' course called 'Christianity Discovered', which is an adapted version of the HTB Alpha Course (see p. 85). Recently, the curate, David Banbury, took this course into the lunch club for 6 weeks for their after-lunch 'entertainment'! It was greatly appreciated, and some have started attending church as a result.

We have seen how many of the suggested '7 keys' for parent and toddler groups can apply for other kinds of group. Very much more study would be needed before they could be billed as anything like 'universal principles'. Nevertheless, the 'keys' may serve as a helpful checklist for the reader.

6 Community Presence – Making Contacts

We continue to look at ways of growing and nurturing the Institutional fringe. Pastoral contacts through the 'occasional offices' will be considered in the next chapter, and we have already looked at community groups. In this chapter, we look at other, more direct ways of creating a fringe, many of which centre round some kind of home visiting. Clearly, this is a more critical issue for some churches than others. Some have so many fringe contacts, the last thing they need is more! For others, though, it is crucial. Some churches need to break out of a ghetto, and create a fringe if they are to start evangelizing. Nothing can happen until they do. What do we mean though by creating a fringe? I believe we mean 2 quite different things: locating those who are open to the gospel, and building up warmth and trust in the community towards the Church.

I shall not theorize too much in this chapter. I shall mainly give examples of those who have done it. But we shall see that creating a fringe is very different in an area with a strong sense of community than in one where people do not know their neighbours. In the latter, like it or not, we are mainly looking for individual fish. In the former, we are trying to influence the shoal!

At the end of the chapter, we shall also look at the tricky issue of how to evangelize the inner fringe. I mean by that, those folk who already see themselves as part of the Church, but whose commitment may be nominal.

Visiting

I need hardly say that visiting is not an effective means of direct evangelism. You cannot bang on doors and instantly convert people! It can be an effective way of creating a large number of contacts, however, but much prayer, skill, and commitment will be needed in following them up. Churches should not launch into visiting schemes too easily. Let me give a few examples of churches where it has worked.

☐ Conisbrough is a mining town in South Yorkshire with a high level of community feeling. It consists of about 4,000 homes, many of them on council estates. St Peter's Anglican church is situated in the old village which forms a centre to the community. The parish has experienced considerable renewal and growth in recent years under the vicar, Ian Chisholm. The church now has about 500 members, most unusual in this kind of area.

One source of the growth was a prayer visiting scheme instituted by the church's evangelist, David Sherwin. The thrust of this was 'prayer, care, and share'. Members were encouraged first to pray for their neighbours, then to care for them in practical ways, and finally to share the gospel. It is not possible to give a number to the people who were influenced by this approach, but there is no doubt it created a considerable 'fringe' of people who were open to talking about the gospel and coming to church or to special events.[1]

The success of the Conisbrough approach depended on having a significant number of spiritually alive church members already living in the parish. What could a smaller church, in a resistant community, do?

☐ St Nathaniel's, Platt Bridge, near Wigan, were guided by God to use an unusual approach. Using a 'community prayer map', the church arranged to pray for 2 or 3 streets in their neighbourhood each week. On Mondays a leaflet was put through all the doors of the relevant streets, talking about local needs, explaining that the congregation were praying for them, and saying that the clergy and some others would be walking down their street praying during Tuesday lunch time, a time when many children and adults would be about. People were invited to meet them and give needs for prayer. The result was 2-fold. There were exciting cases of answered prayer, sometimes leading to people being converted. Also there was a major change in the way the church was seen by the local community – as far more caring and involved.

I researched this case 3 years ago. At that time, 80 adults had been converted over the previous 4 years, mainly through 'Saints Alive' enquirers' groups. Not all had stuck, but the number is considerable in a hard area. Brian Gregory, the vicar at that time, did not feel it possible to quantify the effect of the prayer walking, but he was sure its influence had been considerable. In particular, it had created a better relationship with a community which had previously seen the church as irrelevant. The scheme has developed since those days, but I have included it in its original form. It was such an effective way for a church with few manpower resources to cover a lot of ground.

I have come across several prayer visiting schemes during my research. Most of them involve systematic knocking on doors, asking people if they would like prayer. In some areas it works well with a very high percentage of people responding. In others, there is little or no interest. It tends to work best in UPA areas, where there is a real sense of need, and people value the church showing concern. I have not found cases of it working well in the more middle-class areas of South East England, where 'a man's home is his castle'.

It is tempting to assume that the churches which will have most contact with their local communities will be the long-established denominations. This is not always true. Some of the New Churches see themselves as operating on the Osmosis model. Ichthus Christian Fellowship was founded in 1974 in South East London. It began as a small church, but now forms a network of many congregations, with a strong commitment to social action as well as evangelism. Ichthus, Deptford Park, is one of those congregations.

☐ Ichthus Christian Fellowship, Deptford Park, was founded in 1991 when a home group from a nearby Ichthus congregation felt God was calling them to evangelize their local area. Deptford Park itself is inner city, mainly UPA, with little sense of community. It is racially diverse and quite mixed with a smattering of young professionals. The congregation has grown to involve around 100 people including children in 1994.

The church is unusual in that the largest source of contacts has been door-to-door visiting. The principle has not been to give invitations to church or to explicitly evangelistic events, but to try to discover what local residents themselves would like to do. A team visited with a questionnaire which included a whole range of possible activities. The results were recorded to provide a base for inviting in the future. It was often necessary to invite 30 or 40 people to get 4 or 5.

Successful events have included Easter egg hunts in a park or garden, with 300 children and 70 adults attending over 2 days; inviting men in to watch the World Cup on the TV; men's *Christian* football followed by a visit to the pub; street pancake parties arranged by home groups; free barbecues, bonfire parties, kids' outings and the like. Ichthus, Deptford Park, always seem to go the extra mile. When they go carol singing, for several consecutive nights, they give away mince pies! They arrange 'kids' clubs' with games, races, and prizes at school holidays and half-terms. There is a weekly club for the elderly, and one for mums and toddlers too. There is a youth club (called DNA) and the Lifeboat, a kids' club which meets after school. They also arrange what they call 'helping hand' and 'needing hand'. This might include tidying up old people's gardens, and they would involve unemployed, young men from the area as well as members of the fellowship. In the latter case, they do not hide their 'lights under bushels', but borrow tools from neighbours, which at least means the neighbours know what is going on!

The purpose of all this, of course, is Presence evangelism. In an area where the church has a poor image, as people meet Christians and find that they are normal but loving and with an extra dimension to their lives, it is not surprising that some of them start to ask questions.

This kind of approach requires a great deal of work! Not only is the organization of such events time-consuming; there is a massive amount of follow-up to be done in people's homes. This is only possible because Ichthus, Deptford Park, has working alongside it a team of 5 full- or part-time workers.

They believe that effectiveness and teamwork go together. They have found support in a number of ways – from partners, by taking in lodgers, and by financial support from friends through a trust.

The leaders, Barney and Shirley Skrentny, feel that, as a church, they are better at evangelism than pastoring, which can be immensely demanding in the inner city. So far, over 50 unchurched people have started to attend church, but not all have stayed. Nevertheless, around 20 folk have been baptized and are now involved in the church in a most difficult area.

I have given 3 very different cases involving different amounts of commitment by the church. My point is that the approach taken to door-to-door visiting can and should vary with the type of area and style of church. Other approaches are possible too. Many churches have used street warden schemes, where church members look out for 'for sale' signs coming down and greet newcomers with a 'welcome pack' including helpful local details as well as an invitation to church. It is well known that people are most open to something new following a change in their life pattern, such as a move. The possibilities of carol singing should not be ignored. One Anglican church sent out several teams on the same evening and invited people back to the hall for mince pies and coffee at 9 p.m. with community carol singing and drama. A good number turned up.

Finally, lest it should be thought that a low-key and indirect approach is the only way, let me finish with the example of an Anglican church near Newcastle. The church is in the catholic tradition. Church members visit around 350 houses each year having distributed a letter from the vicar which, in essence, asks one question: 'Do you want to become a Christian?' Only a few respond, but there are always some. The visitors introduce them to the course Good News Down the Street (see p. 81). This year, six people are being confirmed as a result.

Church Magazines

One much neglected way of both warming the community and also identifying receptive people is through literature. There are two approaches to this. The first is by locating and keeping in touch with folk who feel drawn towards the church as an institution through a parish magazine.

☐   Holy Trinity, Stroud, is an Anglican church of moderate catholic church-manship, situated in a country town. There is a stable population, and many have been married in the church or have other links. The parish magazine is of good quality, and includes features of local interest. As an experiment it was decided to visit 100 homes a month, giving free copies of the magazine and inviting subscriptions. To their amazement, 20 to 30 homes a month took out a subscription. After about 15 months the church ran out of distributors!

The church magazine approach will only work where people still have a sense of the church being 'their church'. In many areas the church is seen as boring and irrelevant, and literature will need to relate more directly to people's interest in God. Robert Beale, a tabloid journalist and a Christian, argues that there is very little in most church magazines to interest those who are not church members. He suggests that it is usually best to produce a separate outreach magazine, which need only go out 2 or 4 times a year. Several churches which are doing this have noticed an improved attitude towards the church as a result. Robert runs a service called Release Nationwide which provides material quarterly to help churches produce lively and interesting outreach material.[2]

Advertising

We all know of the immense power of advertising. One of the difficulties for churches, though, is that very often our catchment area does not easily coincide with media availability. In some areas churches are combining now to advertise on the radio, and even on television, at Christmas. This appears to be effective. Are there ways, though, in which the local church can make use of advertising?

Many churches, of course, distribute leaflets advertising Christmas and Easter services. It works better in some areas than others. In truth, apart from this, I have come across very little. Let me share the two small nuggets I have in my bag.

☐ Christ the Rock Church in Yate, north of Bristol, is a church with a great commitment to mission, both overseas and at home. Their local evangelism operates on the Stepping-Stones model, and members are encouraged to invite friends to a range of activities. In order to raise its profile, the church had attractive badges prepared. These were not the usual tin ones, but stylish and quite expensive machine stitched badges. These are very popular amongst the congregation and many of the children have them on their canvas school bags. I am not sure to what extent this was planned, but one can well imagine people asking about the badge, thereby giving an opportunity to talk about the church and possibly to invite people to an event.

The next church is 'something else'! The approach taken to advertising reflects the minister's personality, and it amounts to creating a shift in the whole way the church is seen in the community. I cannot imagine what most other churches could do that would be comparable, but I shall include it in a little detail as it may challenge some of our cosy churchiness.

☐   Church on the High Road, is an Elim Pentecostal church in Willesden, an inner city area in North London with a very high ethnic population. It has grown fast. When Paul Sinclair arrived as minister 5 years ago, the congregation consisted of 12 West Indian women. There are now around 125 members.

In the early days, growth came through an emphasis on fellowship events, drawing in family members and friends. Once the church had grown to around 30 or so, the emphasis changed. Paul deliberately targeted Africans, of whom there were many in the area, with special African evenings and also African guest preachers. There was a major emphasis on 'power ministry' with healing and words of knowledge, even in normal services. Nowadays, much of the prayer for healing is done by members of the congregation, often outside services, but in those days, it was done largely by the minister at the front.

A third phase was to draw in white people who now comprise around 20% of the congregation, even though they are only represented 3% in the area. 'Power' ministry is still an attraction, and many white people come for help with healing and prophetic ministry.

Church on the High Road is a classic Web church. It has few mid-week groups and activities, and most people are brought to services by friends. Some, however, come through another route. Paul Sinclair believes in the importance of advertising.

On one occasion the church paid for a full-page advertisement in a local paper. This was written as an article by the church about itself! Most striking though are the very large posters outside the building. One of these was modelled on a John Player cigarette advertisement 'Black is also available in white', though the church advertisement ran 'John's Prayer Special – Black is also available in white', and included a photograph of the white minister with his black congregation. The point was to impress on white people they were welcome too! Another poster included a massive picture of Clint Eastwood holding a six-shooter. The wording said 'Come to church, "Make my day!" '
Paul found himself engaged in some good-natured correspondence with Clint Eastwood's solicitor for using Clint's image without permission, and this came to the attention of the press and even TV. Newspapers delighted in headlines like 'Dirty Harry Guns for Pastor Paul!' It gained the church massive publicity in the daily, as well as local newspapers. Another Clint Eastwood poster, also with a massive picture, said 'We welcome the Good, the Bad and the Ugly!'

The newspapers which took up the 'Come to church, "Make my day!" ' story included the *Daily Mirror*, the *Sun* and the *Daily Star*. Many Willesden people read these newspapers. Paul had somehow managed to break through the respectable strait-jacket which can so often insulate the church from ordinary people. Some people in Willesden at least have got the message that the Church on the High Road is in touch with real life; and you don't have to leave your sense of humour behind when you go in! I expect most of us would like to get across such a message, though, for my part, I don't know how I will match Clint Eastwood!

Open-Air Services and Events

A third way of making contact with the wider community is through open-air services and events. Most church social events, if they are for outsiders at all, are for friends of church members. These will be considered in chapter 9. What we are looking at in this section are 'big splash' events which the local community will come to purely because they are advertised. Such events are few and far between, and it is fairly obvious that there is no chance of making them work unless there is a fair sense of community in the area.

Villages are the most obvious places where this kind of thing can work. Even the harvest supper may draw a fair crowd of non-church people. 'Urban villages', too, should not be neglected. Street parties can be successful in areas of terraced housing where many people know each other. When Ichthus Christian Fellowship are planning to start a new local area congregation, they always try to organize a street party, a fireworks display, or some such event to which all the local people can be invited. The aim is primarily to let people know that the church exists. Anything beyond this is a bonus.

How should a church decide whether to commit resources to organizing this kind of event? In my view, the answer is simple. In many areas such events simply will not work; but where they will work, they are a highly efficient way of making contact with a large number of people. One event organized by Conisbrough parish church during its period of rapid growth was a flower festival attended by 3,000 people. Clearly, they could never have covered that many homes by door-to-door visiting! David Sherwin, who had just arrived as the church's evangelist, 'loitered with intent' and picked up 75 useful local names to visit – which makes the point that, for all such 'contact events', much of the value is wasted if there is no one to do the follow-up.

Open air services are another kind of 'Profile evangelism'. They are not for everyone. Two obvious requirements before they have a chance of succeeding are a suitable location, such as a town square; and a church which has people interested in singing, street drama and such activities. One must be realistic about the objectives. It is most unlikely that people will be instantly converted on the street. I have known people persuaded to say a prayer of commitment en route from Boots to Marks and Spencers, but they have not turned up in church on Sunday!

Out of 1,000 new Christians analysed in the research, only 2 had been influenced by an open-air service or event. Does that mean this kind of activity can have no value for evangelism at all? For many churches the answer is 'yes'. Occasionally though, a church seems to have the right resources and approach to make this style of evangelism work.

☐   The Town Church, Sevenoaks, is a New Church in a middle-class commuter town. Richard Maggs, the part-time evangelist, organizes regular 'Open Airs'. Over the last 4 or 5 years about 20 people have become Christians and joined the church as a result of these. In Richard's opinion, there are 3 key requirements for such events to be successful. They normally need to be led by a trained and experienced person. There needs to be a support group of, say, 20 people to talk to people and follow them up, possibly by meeting for a drink and a chat, or providing transport to church. Finally, they need to be organized with sufficient regularity, possibly monthly, to enable the team to build up their skills. People who come to faith through open-air services have very often been prepared by God in some way beforehand. Possibly, they are at a point of crisis in their lives, or maybe someone close to them has recently become a Christian.

Opening Up the Church

We are thinking in this chapter of ways of building up an Institutional fringe. The fact is, though, however many contacts we make, it will be to no avail if the church seems closed and exclusive to those who come. Many of these folk will already see themselves as Christians, whatever we may think, and their antennae will quickly detect any subtle sense of 'us and them'. Many evangelical churches have a problem in this regard. Our keenness to 'get people saved' can have the reverse effect. People sense it in all kinds of subtle ways, and, particularly in the Osmosis style of church, it can lose the fringe. Catholic and liberal churches can have an opposite problem. Some are so open that the element of challenge is played down. It can result in a low-commitment church.

How can we preserve the church's integrity as the people of God, and at the same time keep open? To borrow a term used in secular management, we need a 'loose–tight' approach. We should be 'tight' in those areas which are central to our mission, but 'loose' at all other times. One application of this is in deciding whether people who are uncommitted spiritually should be asked to take on jobs in the church. Naturally, responsibilities such as preaching, leading worship, or being a member of an eldership or church council should be reserved for those who are clearly committed Christians. Other forms of service, though, should be opened up as far as possible to anyone who is willing to help. Practical jobs such as flower arranging, looking after the fabric of the church, or making coffee are splendid ways of helping people to be involved. They will meet other members of the church, and it will help to break down barriers.

One of the developments in the last 30 years which has had great benefits, but which has also made many churches more inward looking, is the rapid growth of home groups. We shall look in chapter 11 at ways of making these less insular and more geared to mission.

One outward looking approach, which can be linked to the home group system, is the development of pastoral visiting schemes. I was astonished to read of one church, in Tottenham, which set out to develop such a scheme to involve the whole congregation.[3] The vicar decided that he was '4,000 visits behind!' There are 2 normal ways of responding to a problem like that. I would probably have put my blinkers on and got on with 'churchy' business. The other approach is to become the 'pastoral vicar', who spends all his time visiting, with the result that other areas suffer. Nicholas Bradbury's radical approach was to start to train people, in small groups, in pastoral care. At one stage, 90 people were involved.

Another church with a pastoral visiting scheme is St Mary's, Storrington, an Anglican church of catholic churchmanship in a small town in Sussex. Forty-five people are involved. The congregation, defined in a very broad way to include the fringe, is divided into groups of 5 to 8. Each leader is given responsibility for keeping in touch with their group. They visit when someone is ill or in need, and also, once a quarter, call on those who do not attend church to give them a 'link' letter containing church news and also some evangelistic content. It is very low-key, but an effective way of keeping in touch with the fringe.

The Inner Fringe

One of the most tantalizing problems facing many ministers is that of helping those who actually attend church services, probably occasionally, possibly even regularly, but seem stuck. While some who previously had no contact with the church may now have a vibrant faith, these souls never quite seem to have 'cottoned on'. It applies particularly in the non-confrontational atmosphere of the Osmosis church. We may see it in different ways theologically. Some of us may believe they are in need of salvation, others that they simply need to be warmed up. Either way, the practical issues are not so different. How can we help them forward?

In the research, of the 1,000 people whom the ministers felt had become Christians in the last 5 years, 116, approximately 11%, were either already regular church attenders or came from the long-term fringe (appendix 2, table A6). Most of them, not surprisingly, were from Osmosis-style churches. How were they reached? I cannot give the complete answer, but here are 5 suggestions which have come, directly or indirectly, from the research.

First, the overall ministry is important. The three churches with most new Christians coming from the categories we are considering all had reasonably new ministers.

Second, small groups are vital. People will rarely move forward very far simply from attending Sunday services. The minister of one of the 3 churches had helped the 'open fringe' to a fuller commitment by means of gospel challenges in guest services, coupled with enquirers' groups. In another of them, a Lancashire Methodist church of broad-liberal churchmanship, 23 existing churchgoers had recently come into church membership. Most of these were folk who had started coming to church as a result of the children attending Sunday school. It had taken them time to acclimatize themselves, to feel they belonged, but then a church membership class was just what they needed to firm up their commitment. At another Methodist church, an annual 'school of faith' served the same purpose. It is interesting that non-confrontational titles were used for these groups. If instead they had been called 'get saved' groups I wonder how many people would have attended!

This brings us to the third point. In the Osmosis church, one has to be careful of the use of language. The inner fringe do not usually respond well to the suggestion that they may not be Christians! One church using the adult catechumenate (see p. 82) found a good number of these folk were drawn in as sponsors, and they gained just as much as the catechumens.

Particular care needs to be taken if a challenge to commitment is made, for example, during a mission. Those who have attended church for many years may be unlikely to respond if asked to 'become a Christian'. I remember one mission at the start of the dramatic growth at Holy Trinity, Brompton, in London. John Collins, the missioner, asked those who wished to 'take a step forward in or into Christian faith', to kneel at the communion rail. It was acceptable to those with or without church backgrounds. This kind of sensitivity can be specially important, of course, in country areas.

Fourth, I should like to mention an approach which was featured recently in the Church of England Newspaper. How, as a minister, are you to start up worthwhile spiritual conversations with some of the long-term folk we are talking about? One priest, I think from a catholic background, introduced the concept of a 'spiritual MOT' in the run-up to Holy Week. A short questionnaire looking at different points in the Christian life was made available at the back of church, and 51 were returned. All came for a 30-minute interview. Tony Pinchin was strict about the time, though many follow-up interviews were arranged. Over 40 made sacramental confession. 'Discovery of retreats, regular spiritual reading, commitment to weekday eucharists, realistic financial giving and extra work for the church all resulted.'

An even more direct approach is used by Wallace Benn, an Anglican vicar from the evangelical tradition. Wallace works systematically through the electoral role inviting each couple to come and see him for half an hour. They are invited on the basis that, in a big church, that is the only way he can get to know everyone in the congregation. 'I also say that I should like to know how they are getting on spiritually and be of any help to them that I can.' Amazingly, no one has ever refused to come! Wallace always asks 3 questions: when (and if), they became a Christian; how their Christian life is going now; and how they are using their gifts in the Lord's service. One evening a week is given to this activity, which is clearly time-consuming, but it does mean that the vicar makes direct spiritual contact with every member of his electoral role – and that will include the fringe, some of whom have been directed on to 'discovering Christianity' courses.

Fifth, may I say something quite obvious, that hyper-enthusiasts like me need to hear: 'You can't win 'em all.' It seems to me, that the fringe are rather like traffic lights: green, orange, or red. The green lights are the 'open fringe'. Frankly, if they are really open, almost any strategy will do. The orange lights are the people we have been considering. With encouragement and sensitivity as to where they are at in their spiritual journey, they can be helped forward. The red lights have come precisely as far as they want to and no amount of nudging will move them any further. They have their own agenda.

7 Church Services

Gavin Reid has suggested that many people's route to faith is something like this. First, they encounter God's goodness, usually in some way through people. This produces a new openness to God, which results in them starting to attend church, and growing into faith. Thus most people become Christians *after* they have started to attend church. This is in contrast to the model that many evangelicals have in their minds of becoming a Christian first, and then finding a church. Needless to say, the latter does happen. We considered some examples in chapter 5. Nevertheless, it is not the normal route.

Of the new Christians in the churches covered by the first survey, for 70% of women and 74% of men, attending a church service was their first contact with the organization. Clearly this will vary for the different models of church. In the case of a Web church, the usual point of first contact is a service. For a Stepping-Stone church, or one with many community groups, more people will attend other groups or organizations first. Even then, they may well attend a church service fairly soon, even if it is the annual carol service.

Services alone are not usually enough. The two categories of 'general church involvement' and 'special guest services' accounted together for only 25% of the factors bringing people to faith in the first survey (appendix 2, table A7). Nevertheless, attending a service is the usual first step. For one thing, a 'user-friendly' service is often the best thing on offer for an invitation to family or friends. As John Finney puts it in his analysis of the CTE Research, 'There were a few stories of friends who had "led someone to Christ" – but far more stories of people who had invited their friends to come to church'.[1]

Thus a church service is almost certain to be an important step, and probably an early one, in the journey of faith. Yet it is not always an easy one. For many who have never been to church before, particularly men, it can be a positively embarrassing one! Clearly we need to do all we can to make attending church as easy as possible for the enquirer. In this chapter we consider a number of different types of services which have been 'ways in' for many people.

All-Age Family Services

There is a myth that family services pull in a fringe. By 'family service' I mean a service in which the children stay in for the whole time, rather than going out to Sunday school; in which the sermon is usually short with visual aids; and where the children are probably involved in some way in the service. The aim is to get over deep truths in a light and entertaining way. Many, nowadays, prefer the phrase 'all-age service' to 'family service', feeling that the latter phrase can be taken as excluding single or elderly people.

One advantage of this kind of service is that it can give the Sunday school teachers a welcome break, and therefore many churches hold an all-age service once a month.

One of the questions in the surveys was designed to discover whether it is true that family services attract people from the fringe. The answer for the churches in the survey was that, while *weekly* all-age services, and even monthly services held at a different time from the main service, could pull a fringe, monthly services held at the usual service time usually did not.

The average fringe for a family service held at the standard service time was 6 adults (appendix 2, table A5). Even this is an overstatement for most churches, and reduces to 3 if 11 churches are removed from the analysis. These churches have an average adult fringe of 20. I was able to investigate all but one of them, and in each case there was a special reason. In 3 cases, unusually today, there were a good number of unchurched children in the Sunday school. Understandably, when the children were involved in the service, their parents attended. In another case there was a successful mid-week children's club, with the same result. In 4 cases, the church encouraged the congregation particularly to invite friends to the family service, in one case using it as a regular follow-up to a popular annual children's holiday club. In the other 2 churches, the all-age service was used effectively for baptism follow-up and as a link with the parent and toddler club.

The message seems clear. A monthly family service will only bring in a fringe if there is some particular reason why it should. The family service is not an 'Open Door' of its own right. I have found this applies across cultures. It has been suggested to me that in country areas a family service will still be effective, in its own right, in pulling in a fringe. I can only say it does not apply in the churches covered by my surveys.

What *is* true, is that a family service held *at a different service time* can certainly draw people in, and this arrangement often happens in the country. The two churches in the survey which had their monthly all-age service at a different time were rural and semi-rural, and on average they had 31 fringe adults at these services. In each case the normal congregation was elderly, so it is easy to see how the family service drew in extra people. Nevertheless, the difference in average size of fringe, 31 versus 6, is dramatic!

In the case of the weekly family services, it is harder to estimate the size of the fringe from the statistics. When is a weekly attender to be described as 'fringe'? Rather I will demonstrate in some of the case studies below how some churches have used a weekly family service to bring in many new people.

I have so far said nothing about the uniformed organizations, which can be an important element in many monthly family services. Parade services do, indeed, bring in a fringe. In addition to the extra children, the uniformed leaders and, often, good numbers of parents attend the parade services. In my research, they amounted to an average of 18 extra adults. I do not decry this in any way. We shall see below that few of these adults become Christians as a result, but the prime purpose of a parade service is for the children. Who knows what the long-term result will be. My point is simply that we should be realistic about what is happening in the monthly family service and that their power to pull in a fringe of their own accord is limited.

☐ St Augustine's, Bradford, is an Anglican church situated in a UPA area, near the city centre. The church has experienced considerable renewal and growth in recent years. The modern church building, which seats around 150, also houses a coffee shop. The church has 2 morning services each week: a Holy Communion service at 9.30 a.m. with an active children's Sunday school; and the 11.15 a.m. 'Sunday Special' which is a lively all-age family service.

The Sunday Special is targeted towards unchurched people. The length is kept to 50 minutes. The style is snappy , with 'bouncy singing', quizzes and competitions. Every effort is made to keep it relevant to the culture of ordinary people. For example, an early sermon series was on the theme 'Bart Simpson meets Jesus'. For many, it is the first service they come to.

Sunday Special was launched in 1991, with 50 adults coming as a core group from the original morning service. Initially, only a small number of fringers, possibly 15, started to attend. Eighteen months later, attendance was about 75 adults, most of whom were fringe or visitors. Very few, by then, were from the original core group. This success was achieved by having a weekly service which could be enjoyed by unchurched people. A monthly family service would never have produced growth in the same way.

☐ St Andrew's, Bedford, is an Anglican church in the liberal catholic tradition in a suburban area. The church holds a quiet 8 a.m. communion service, and a 10.30 a.m. sung eucharist with a mainly elderly congregation but also some young adults, attracting congregations of around 45 and 90 adults respectively. Both these services have experienced only modest growth. The 9 a.m. family service, on the other hand, has tripled from 65 adults 10 years ago, to around 220 (140 adults and 80 children) in 1994. This service is also a eucharist, though it is kept to around 50 minutes and the sermon is very short, around 5 to 7 minutes, with visual aids. The steady growth testifies to the fact that it is a helpful way in for many from the church's large fringe. Many of the committed also find it sustains them spiritually.

☐ St Andrew's, Goldsworth Park, is a large estate of predominantly private housing on the edge of Woking, a London commuter town in Surrey. The church has a modern building, with its own coffee house, in the centre of the estate next to the Waitrose car park.

The 9.30 a.m. Sunday Special service, has around 45 adults and 30 or 40 children, mostly below the age of 7. Few had strong previous church links and nearly all of them have come as a result of baptism enquiries for the children. They mostly come as couples. The service lasts just over half an hour, and is led on a rota basis by different lay teams.

I attended a service. It was a classic case of the homogeneous group principle working well. It was easy to see how the new couples felt at home, in a modern building, with not too large a group of mainly young couples like themselves. They actually *believed* that the others did not mind if their baby cried! The service consisted of a mixture of songs led by a small guitar group, prayers, a reading, and a short talk for which the children came to the front. Some weeks, I understand, there is drama. Even though the service is led by lay people, it does need support by the clergy, and it was some years until there were an adequate number of lay teams. Nevertheless, I did not feel there was anything being done which most congregations, provided they had couples with children of the right age, could not achieve. Many of the couples move on to the 10.45 a.m. service, which has a Sunday School, when the children reach around 7 years old.

It could be argued that the teaching cannot be very adequate for enquiring Christian adults, given the length of the service and the age of the children present. Nevertheless, many join home groups fairly soon after starting to attend. Furthermore, Andrew Knowles, the vicar when I researched the service and who started Sunday Special, used it flexibly. Occasionally he took the adults out for solid teaching. During one series looking at the 10 commandments, he took the men out on their own when it came to the subject of adultery! The adults were only too happy on such occasions to leave the toddlers upstairs having a 'praise-up'.

☐ Our Lady of the Immaculate Conception is a Roman Catholic church in a new parish in the Surrey Docks in South East London. The congregation started meeting in the church school 5 years ago, but now has a building of its own.

The morning mass lasts an hour, and children who have been confirmed, normally those 7 or 8 and over, stay in for the whole service. The sermon is kept to about 5 minutes, and the children are involved, for example, bringing up the gifts for the communion. There is an informal atmosphere which helps young families feel at home. Numbers at the service have grown from 50 to 250 over the last 5 years.

I must confess, the growth potential of weekly family services has been an eye-opener to me. I have given 4 different case studies to emphasize the point that a weekly family service can bring sustained growth in a variety of cultures and church traditions. Furthermore, as the Goldsworth Park case demonstrates, much can be achieved by lay people. There is hope for busy ministers!

The next case is set in a rural context, and shows how a monthly service can be effective if it is held at a different time from the main service. As with Goldsworth Park, it is lay led.

☐   Barton Mills[2] is a Suffolk country village. A few years ago, the Sunday school teachers approached Graham Hedger, the vicar at the time, and said 'We have people coming to Sunday school who find it more interesting and exciting than church. What are you going to do about it?' At that stage, 3 clergy and 2 leaders were dealing with 12 churches, and the prospect of another service filled him with horror so he told them to find a solution themselves. The answer was called 'Sunday Night Special'. It took place at 5 p.m. on Sunday afternoon, once a month in the church rooms, and was followed by an informal tea. The service was open to all ages but geared primarily to those with young children. The format was informal and simple: plenty of choruses led initially on an electronic keyboard, and later by a growing worship group. Most of the teaching came in small snatches of about 2 to 3 minutes.

From the first meeting of 40 people, the service grew to a peak of 100 attending regularly and nearly 200 for festivals. They now meet in the church. Numbers have dropped a little recently as a result of other less formal services being introduced at Barton Mills and in other nearby villages. The leadership are wondering if a service geared to unchurched adults might be right for the future. Most of those who come are still fringe folk, and about half are from the village which has a population of only 700.

Why is the weekly family service, in particular, so successful at drawing people in? I believe there are 3 reasons.

First, many unchurched people feel uneasy about the children going out to Sunday school. I am sure the established church children far prefer it to most family services, but it is another matter for a young child who does not know the others in the group, and for parents who already feel uneasy. This applies doubly if the visiting family are in any way different culturally from most of the congregation. A family service is, hopefully, relaxed, short, and understandable. It does much to break down the barriers.

Second, the homogeneous group principle can apply. We saw this at Goldsworth Park. Young couples will understandably feel most relaxed in the presence of other young couples. This can affect the whole atmosphere of the service as well. In the usual monthly family service, where many adults without children are present, it can be much harder to 'get them going'.

Third, the difficulty of the monthly service is that people forget! Unless someone is very keen to come, they will simply not remember that on the third Sunday they need to get out of bed early and drag the children off to church!

The weekly family service has, in some areas, an enormous power for pulling in an open fringe. Nevertheless, it would be facile to deny that it has its disadvantages. Not every minister is gifted in this kind of communication, and there may not be suitable lay leaders available. I, personally, enjoy leading and preaching at family services, but I must admit I would be daunted at the prospect of it every week! What is more, however hard you try, it is not possible to give adequate biblical teaching on all subjects in a service with young children present. In my own evangelical tradition there is a saying 'sermonets make Christianets!' Churches try to get round this problem in different ways. Some give considerable emphasis to teaching in the mid-week home groups, others encourage attendance at the evening service. Perhaps the best solution is when families move on to a different morning service as their children get old enough, and their own needs for teaching deepen.

The disadvantages are real, but they need to be set against the enormous potential of the weekly family service as an open door for evangelism, especially for a church with little existing fringe. We have seen how, in most churches, there is little natural flow from either pram services or the uniformed organizations to regular churchgoing. The only cases I have come across where this has happened successfully have been weekly family services. What is more, they avoid the difficulty of moving people over the next hurdle, from monthly to weekly attendance. As Martyn Cripps, vicar of St Cuthbert's, Fulwood, Preston, a church with a very successful weekly family service, said to me when admitting the difficulties I have just mentioned: 'All I know is, people regularly come to faith in the family service.'

Let me make 4 practical suggestions for running a family service to pull in the fringe. Most of them apply whether the all-age service is weekly or monthly.

First, clarify the target group. Is it families with very young children, or is it the junior age group? The target group will clearly influence the style of service and the means of recruiting.

Second, look for a link strategy. Even with a weekly service, families will need to come from somewhere! The key will usually lie with the children. The New Life Church in Harrow run occasional 'praise parties' to draw in friends of the children, who give out invitations at school. A good number have come, often with parents. These are well planned events with drama and lively music, and are popular with the children. The church feels it is important to use a name which the children relate to, such as a 'party', rather than a 'service', which may mean little to many.

The Lantern Church, in Canford Magna, near Bournemouth, runs a monthly Saturday morning club for children in the 6 to 11 year age range on the day before the monthly family service. This involves craft work, and also a lively time of worship. Clearly, if the children at a club such as this can be organized to do some drama or some other item the next morning, it will encourage adult family members to come to church with them.

Third, if you are considering starting a weekly all-age service, it may be appropriate to start with a monthly service, but at a different service time, to give some feel for the atmosphere there will be with mainly families present.

Fourth, if the service is to be monthly, regular distribution of invitations to the fringe is essential. In my own experience it can double the number of such folk who attend.

The Occasional Offices

The 'occasional offices' of baptisms, weddings, and funerals are a fertile source of new people coming in, particularly for Anglican and Church of Scotland churches, but also for Methodists in some areas, and of course Roman Catholics. Infant baptisms are the most fertile source of the 3 (appendix 2, table A6). They account for 9% of new adults coming in for the churches covered by the first survey, and this figure was considerably higher for the Osmosis churches in the survey. Weddings and funerals between them brought in $2\frac{1}{2}$% and 3% of new adults, respectively. The funerals figure may seem low compared with other estimates. For example, in the CTE Research, bereavement was considered an important factor in a gradual process for 9% of people.[3] The figures from the first survey are understandably lower as they refer to something more specific, namely people coming to faith as a direct result of infant baptisms, funerals, and weddings carried out by the church in question. Harder to explain, the CTE Research only gives having a child baptized as a source of becoming a Christian for 5% of people. I am not sure how to explain the difference. It may be that my sample of churches, all members of the British Church Growth Association, were more 'on the ball' than average churches in this respect. The point remains that for churches that are alert to the possibilities, the opportunities are considerable.

INFANT BAPTISMS

There can have been few subjects to raise more theological controversy than infant baptism. Many, of course, take a Baptist position that there is no justification for it at all. Pedobaptists usually justify it in one of two ways. Some, after St Augustine, believe that a child can be baptized on the basis of the faith of the Church. This position is taken by many of catholic persuasion. Others take the view that children can only be baptized on the basis of their parents' faith. This is justified by means of covenant theology, after Calvin and others. This author admits to the latter view, which is taken by most modern evangelicals. Not surprisingly, those who justify infant baptism on the basis of the faith of the Church normally tend towards an open baptismal policy, whereas the covenant theology people would be happier to baptize only the children of at least one Christian parent. In practice these two 'pure' positions are normally modified for all sorts of reasons, pragmatic and theological. Many, including this author, believe that a *very* tight policy can have disastrous results in terms of alienating the local community. Most clergy fall somewhere between an extreme open or indiscriminate position on one hand and a very tight position on the other.

Many thousands of pages have been written on the theological arguments. I do not argue either position here, simply because others better qualified have done it elsewhere.[4] My modest contribution is to try to throw some light on the question of what works evangelistically in practice. My conclusions must be tentative. They are somewhat impressionistic, and are based on around 20 telephone conversations, with mainly Anglican ministers. The number of variables are so great that it would be difficult to do much more than this.

In order to form an effective baptism policy, decisions are needed in 3 areas: the preparation course, the nature of the service at which the baptism will be held, and which the family will later be encouraged to attend; and the follow-up.

The biggest question in the preparation is how 'closed-ended' it should be. Churches run courses ranging from one evening to 7 or even more sessions, and, generally speaking, the longer the course, the greater the expectation that the couple will become Christians before the baptism. Most of the tailor-made baptism courses, however, some of which use video, are fairly open-ended. We shall discuss in due course whether they are missing an opportunity.

The baptism itself can take place at a range of different services: at an all-age service with many children; at the main morning Holy Communion service; or at a special baptism service on a Sunday afternoon, at which only the baptism family and their friends are present. As far as the Church of England is concerned, this latter approach is discouraged by the canons, but, in parishes with a very large number of infant baptisms, the clergy sometimes feel that it is necessary in the interests of both the normal congregation and the baptism family. By having the service in the afternoon the talk and style of service can be geared to the needs of the family.

In my opinion, the baptism service itself is hardly an issue as far as evangelism is concerned. Most couples are very happy with the service. What is more critical is the nature of the service they will later be encouraged to join. We shall see some examples in the cases below.

Follow-up can take many forms. At one stage, I believed that the most important thing in evangelizing baptism couples would be to provide a link with a similar-aged couple in the congregation. This was on the basis of the Three-Stranded Cord. I reasoned that baptism enquirers are usually at an early stage on the road to faith, and in such cases personal friendship is usually the most important strand in the cord. What I had failed to take into account was that we are dealing with an unusual faith journey. The couple will have at least a nominal faith, and will have made formal promises about church attendance. This can affect the follow-up strategy.

Churches use a number of approaches to the follow-up. Some do, indeed, provide links with members of the congregation. Others arrange additional teaching. Yet others try to keep in touch by organizing baptism reunion services or teas, and maybe delivering annual birthday cards for the first few years. I can see the point of this. As a new father myself, I have to acknowledge that the first months or even years of a child's life are not the easiest times to start attending church! Keeping the contact warm until the child reaches an age to attend Sunday school may well be a valid strategy.

I do not claim to have the final answer on any of these issues, though I believe I have some insights to share from the research. These will make more sense once we have looked at some case studies.

☐   St Peter and St Paul, Hucknall, is an Anglican church of mixed evangelical and catholic tradition, serving a large housing estate on the west side of Hucknall, some miles north of Nottingham. The church stands amongst the older, largely council, housing, but other parts of the estate are owner-occupied. The 10 a.m. morning service is always a parish eucharist, and about 120 people attend, nearly all from the estate. A high proportion of the local residents are young couples with children, and this is reflected by the fact that two-thirds of the newcomers into the fellowship over a recent 5-year period have been baptism enquirers.

Preparation consists of one discussion evening attended by several couples. In addition they are expected to attend church at least twice. After this, if they still wish to proceed, a date is fixed for the baptism. At one stage there were 3 preparation meetings and only one visit to church, but experience of the morning worship proved a better communicator in the end than extra meetings. During the preparation evening, when the promises are explained, it is suggested that 'being within the family of the church' should mean attendance at the morning eucharist at least once a month.

In the opinion of Tim Haggis, the team vicar, the flavour of the church worship is an important ingredient in the church's success in keeping baptism enquirers. The age range of the congregation is quite young, there are many children, and the music is lively and varied in style. Most important, in the congregation they meet other people like themselves and sometimes people they already know. Welcoming the baby and its parents is taken seriously, and a Polaroid snap is taken after the baptism service and displayed at the back of the building to help the congregation recognize them again.

For follow-up, the church run groups for exploring Christian faith further, but Tim Haggis finds that the worship itself is the most important factor. People soon feel they belong.

The church has about 25 enquiries and perhaps 20 baptisms a year. Of these, in recent years, 20% have become fully committed Christians and church members, and a further 25% come to church occasionally.

Further details on this case can be found in the book *Infant Baptism and the Gospel* by Colin Buchanan.[5]

☐ St Paul's, Kingston Hill, is an Anglican church in middle-class commuter land in Surrey. There are around 30 baptism enquiries a year and, say, 24 baptisms. Of these 25% stick. Of last year's baptism couples, 3 are now clearly committed, and 3 more come occasionally to church and are also involved in various ways, such as helping with coffee or attending a toddler group. The approach is different from Hucknall, in that baptism preparation is carried out in the home by one of a team of lay couples. Enquirers are expected to come to at least one service, and then to have at least 2 preparation evenings in their home.

Like Hucknall, there are many young children and families in the church. The congregation is quite large, normally around 250 in all, and the service lasts about an hour and a quarter. There is a monthly family service. At present there is no planned follow-up. Nevertheless, the link with the lay couples is clearly an important factor in helping welcome people and get them involved.

☐ St Anne's, Chasetown, is situated in an urban area of mixed private and council housing, about 12 miles north of Birmingham. The vicar, Michael Wooderson, is the author of the well-known course for enquirers: *Good News Down the Street*. (This is a 6-week course led by lay people in an enquirer's own home. We consider it further on p. 81). There are about 120 adults usually in the morning service. The church has an open baptism policy. Preparation involves 2 sessions. First, there is a visit to get to know the couple or parent involved. This is followed by an evening with both parents and godparents to discuss the promises they will make and to run through the service.

The most important factor in leading people to Christian commitment is that a little while after the baptism, couples are offered the chance to do the course *Good News Down the Street* in their home. This will lead to confirmation for those who wish it. A routine, helpfully worded letter is sent to them[6] together with a video.[7] The course is described in the letter as 'a series of informal discussions about the Christian faith, which will give you a better understanding of what Christians believe and help you to give your child the Christian upbringing you promised'. St Anne's has around 30 to 40 baptisms a year, and nearly 40 parents have come to faith in this way in the last 5 years.

What can be deduced from these and other cases? I offer the following suggestions.

First, the nature of the regular Sunday service couples are to be

invited to attend is crucial. It is more important than I had realized. At
one stage, after I had visited Goldsworth Park (see p. 61), I came to the
conclusion that a very short service was necessary. Several people at my
own church had suggested that couples with babies could not cope with
more than an hour, even with a well-equipped crèche. I see the point,
but in Hucknall and also Kingston Hill, the service lasts 75 minutes. My
cautious suggestion is that whether there are a large number of other
young couples present is even more important than length of service. It
is a classic case of the homogeneous unit principle. Only in such a
setting will many couples really feel relaxed about their baby crying. In
a service where, for example, many of the congregation are elderly or
single, I wonder if churches should not consider starting a family service
at a separate time.

Clearly, the welcome is vital. Many baptism couples will feel ill at
ease on coming to a church, and practical ways of making them feel at
home are worth their weight in gold. The taking of a Polaroid snap, as
they do at Hucknall, seems an excellent idea. One church, St Edmond's,
Tyesley, built a crèche at the back of the church looking like a local
castle. It showed that small children were being taken seriously.

What about the preparation? Should it aim to lead people to
committed Christian faith before the baptism? I have come down on the
side of the fence which says 'no'. Michael Wooderson helped me to see
this. The course Good News Down the Street is intended to be an open-
ended look at Christianity, but if it is done before the baptism,
particularly if there is any expectation of a 'decision for Christ', it can
create an inappropriate kind of pressure. Furthermore, if everyone is
made to do the course, a high percentage of the couples will not feel able
to respond positively at the end. This can be disheartening for the team,
and may produce some bad feeling. The same applies with any course
which places a high expectation of full Christian commitment before the
baptism. We must be realistic about where people are in their faith
journey, and in my judgement this will often involve 'holding our fire' –
though I can appreciate the viewpoint of those ministers who are
unwilling to accept the degree of compromise in the baptism service
which this approach can involve.

What, then, is the most effective form of preparation? I have no hard
evidence. Naturally, one will wish to be as welcoming as possible, while
explaining the nature of the commitment the parents and godparents
are making. (Though if they *really* understood the promises they would
become Christians! We are usually talking about partial understanding
at this stage, hoping to stimulate enough interest for them to get
involved in the follow-up.) Videos are a popular resource. Many
churches feel the couples will be most relaxed if seen in their own home.
Others favour meeting as a group, and in some cases the friendships
made in the group can encourage them to start coming to church. One

or two churches felt food or good refreshments were a vital ingredient for helping people relax, particularly if they depended on just one session. Follow-up is where I am a little puzzled. I cannot see why some of the churches who are most successful in drawing people in through baptisms are so slow to 'close the sale'! Michael Wooderson is at a considerable disadvantage in terms of his building compared with Hucknall or Goldsworth Park. He describes it in his book as 'vast, cold, damp and badly lit, full of dark-stained pitch pine pews and furniture all set off by faded paint work!'[8] It has improved vastly since then, but even in the early days the one simple expedient of asking the couples afterwards if they would like to do Good News Down the Street produced the results. Am I missing something? It seems such a natural solution. Admittedly, some churches invite recent baptism couples to their next 'basics' group; but surely, for couples with comparatively new babies, a course in their own homes must be best, must it not?

WEDDINGS

Opportunities for evangelization can be more restricted with weddings, as many newly married couples do not go on to live in the parish or area where they are married. For those who stay, however, a helpfully run wedding can forge the start of a relationship with the minister which may be renewed in due course when the couple bring their children for baptism or dedication.

One particular group which can be receptive to the gospel at this time are divorced people wanting to remarry. Of the 25 new Christians in the research who were first contacted through a wedding, at least half were in this category. Such folk can be extremely appreciative of a minister who will remarry them after they have, in their eyes, been rejected elsewhere. I appreciate, of course, that many clergy are unable to marry in these circumstances, and I make no judgement whatever on those on either side of the fence.

There are 3 areas to be considered in evangelization: marriage preparation; the content of church services which couples may attend; and maintaining the contact afterwards. I do not include the wedding service itself. Like most ministers, I do what I can to weave in the gospel in the sermon, but the couples seem to have other matters on their mind! Three case studies follow which are largely self-explanatory.

☐ Hockliffe Street Baptist Church in Leighton Buzzard receives many requests for marriage from divorced people who are unable to marry in the local Anglican churches. They are usually living together and completely unchurched. Norman Barr, the minister, runs regular marriage preparation classes over a period of 5 weeks. He limits each class to 6 couples. For materials he uses a mixture of *Marriage in Mind*, produced by CPAS, and *The Adam and Eve Factor*, a video from International Films. All 6 couples from the last group committed their lives to Christ, and all are now at least partly involved in the church. This was not unusual. These couples are at a time in their lives where they are receptive to the gospel.

Norman Barr believes there are 2 key factors in the success of this approach. First, a helpful relationship is built up during the class, which includes some gospel content. He then visits each couple at home before the wedding and, if it feels right to do so, he asks them if they would like him to pray with them to become Christians. It has to be said that Norman has a particular evangelistic gifting. Nevertheless, his advice to others is to trust the Holy Spirit and yourself. While it is quite wrong to try to pressurize those who are not open, too many people hesitate when in fact the door is wide open.

Afterwards, couples are encouraged to keep attending church, and a good proportion attend the 'pastor's classes', which are preparation for baptism and church membership.

☐   St Michael's, Gospel Lane, is an Anglican church set in a council estate in East Birmingham. The vicar, Rob Johnson, is a video enthusiast! For both baptism and wedding preparation he adapts a home grown course lasting 2 or 3 weeks known as 'First Steps'. It is Bible-based, and stories of Jesus are used to lead into discussion on such topics as the real meaning of love. This is a different approach from some marriage preparation courses which concentrate on issues such as finance, communication, and sex! Rob feels that, since most couples are already living together, they already have some knowledge in most of these areas and so favours a Bible-based approach.

The first week's session includes a 10-minute video of the church, including a baptism, a wedding, and interviews with some of the members about what Christian faith means to them. A special feature is that Rob splices in some shots of the couple's own street at the start of the video to make it as personal as possible! The approach works well. The church does not take many weddings, but all 5 couples from last year are still in touch. In fact, wedding couples are their best source of fringe members at the family service.

☐   Arborfield and Barkham are two commuter villages on the edge of Reading. They form a joint Anglican parish. The churches are attractive to wedding couples, and some attend the church for 6 months in order to join the electoral roll so that they may be married in one of the churches. Most are young professionals, who have some affinity with the church, if only for the architecture. David Rowe, the vicar, recommends couples to attend the monthly 'seeker service', which is specifically geared to unchurched people. Many come, and appreciate the services. A good proportion have since come to 'Open to Question' groups, and some have become Christians.

FUNERALS

When I was a curate in Birmingham, I took at least one funeral most weeks. I spoke to more non-Christians then than at any other time. You can imagine that someone as obsessed with evangelism as I am was determined to get across the gospel if I could in a sensitive way. How far could I go? For a time, at each funeral I 'stepped up the gas'! Would they accept it? Each time, to my amazement, the handshakes became even more appreciative as I greeted them on leaving the building. Did they realize I was saying that not everyone, the departed included, would reach heaven? The fact is, they could hear the 'tune', but not the 'words'. They liked the warmth of my message, but could not take in much of the meaning.

Later, as I pondered on the Three-Stranded Cord of Evangelism, I came to see why. Most people attending a funeral were not at a stage in their spiritual journey when gospel teaching was what they particularly needed. They needed 'gospel presence', the love and care of Christians. I saw this happen. Women sometimes came into faith as a result of joining our senior citizens' lunch club, which provided companionship and where there was much love and care.

Does that mean that there is no point in trying to share gospel teaching with bereaved folk? Clearly, one needs to be sensitive. Pastoral needs must be met first. Nevertheless, after a wait of perhaps a month, some churches have found bereaved people will be pleased to join a Christian 'basics' group. In one church, 5 people became Christians in this way in one year.

In some cases, people will start attending church after a funeral, though this seems to depend on local culture. In many parts of the north of England, there is a tradition that the family attend church on the Sunday after the funeral, sometimes even for 3 Sundays. A percentage of these folk find that attending church meets a need in their lives and become Christians as a result.

Let me give 2 cases studies which may be helpful.

☐ St Oswald's, Bidston, is an Anglican church serving UPA council estates near Birkenhead. The vicar when I researched the case was Paul Kirby. Over the 9 years he was there the congregation grew from 8 to around 150. Most of these were not previously Christians, and most, astonishingly, were converted through funeral ministry.

Bidston is an area where there is a strong tradition of attending church after a funeral. Paul Kirby always used to say at the end of the service in the crematorium that there would be a warm welcome at the church service on Sunday, where there would be prayers for the family. A very high percentage came, and some simply kept on coming.

Every year the church held a bereavement service, with tea at 5 p.m. and the service at 6 p.m. 180 letters would be sent out, from which maybe 50 people usually came. It is hard to quantify the effect of this, but it was clearly a worthwhile way of keeping in contact and of meeting a pastoral need at the same time.

☐ St Alban's, Wickersley, is an Anglican church of central tradition serving a suburban village in South Yorkshire. As in Bidston, there is an annual service for the bereaved, held in the evening on All Saints Day. More than 200 attend. For the first time in 1993, a course was launched at this service known as 'Picking up the Pieces'. This was organized and run by Margaret Whipp, a doctor and non-stipendiary minister in the parish.

The course, which lasted 5 weeks, proved a great success. Twelve people came, mainly aged between 30 and 60. It is quite different from anything I have seen before. It contains a mixture of poetry, music, silence and prayer, teaching on grief, reflection on scripture, and discussion of matters both practical and emotional. It was extremely well received. For some it was their first chance really to 'open up' since the funeral. Clearly, the purpose of the course was at least as much pastoral as evangelistic. It is too soon to predict the effect in terms of people coming to faith, but it clearly helped nearly everyone forward on their journey.

Guest and Seeker Services

Traditional guest services are starting to give way to a new and more low-key approach known as a 'seeker service'. By 'guest service' I mean the kind of approach much used by evangelicals over the years where friends are invited to hear a particularly challenging preacher who makes an appeal for Christian commitment at the end of his sermon. I shall leave consideration of this type of service until chapter 9. It is really one of a number of options for Proclamation evangelism, and it will most naturally fit into that chapter. At this stage I simply make the point that, as the water-table of faith in our culture is declining, many are saying that a 'one-off' appeal to commitment is becoming less appropriate.

The term 'seeker service' was scarcely heard in Britain until June 1992 when a large conference was organized in Birmingham to introduce British churches to the approach used by the Willow Creek Community Church. This church is situated in the suburbs of Chicago. The church was founded in 1975 by members of a dynamic youth group who decided to start a church to evangelize their parents' generation. Starting in a cinema, they arranged services, using drama and music, which were designed to appeal, not to Christians, but to unbelievers. The church has grown fast. It now has its own building with a congregation of 17,000, and is the second largest Protestant church in the USA. It sticks to the same philosophy as when it began. The Sunday services are 'targeted' not at Christians, but at enquirers or 'seekers'. A worship service for believers is held mid-week.

The very approach invites questions. Is it 'church' if two-thirds of those present are unbelievers, as at Willow Creek? One could ask the same question of many carol services, but we do not deny their value. Is the word 'seeker' something of a misnomer? Does it provide too linear a picture of people's journey to faith? In many ways, yes. Nevertheless, the approach works dramatically well at Willow Creek, with thousands coming to faith. It is not surprising that it has attracted a lot of interest in Britain.[9]

We need to be clear about one thing. The reason Willow Creek has experienced such dramatic growth is that it is a Web church operating in a large, moderately receptive population. They consider themselves to be a local church, but see their 'parish' as around 300,000 people! The church is quite explicit about its strategy. The way new people are to come is that friends should invite friends. It operates on a Personal fringe. The only way such dramatic and sustained growth could have been achieved was through a Web dynamic operating through a large moderately receptive population. I have no problem about this at all, but it needs to be borne in mind when considering the likely impact in Britain. In chapter 12 we shall see how quite normal differences in such factors as the number of unchurched friends people have, the proportion who live in the catchment area of the church, and their receptivity to the gospel can make the difference between a Web church reaching a plateau at just over 100 or growing to 12,000 in 11 years! The figures, of course, are based on a simplified model. Nevertheless, the relevance when comparing Britain with USA – where people are known to have more friends and contacts, people will travel further to church, and there is a much higher general church attendance and, arguably therefore, gospel receptivity – is obvious.

During my research I have come across a large number of churches of different churchmanship which have been experimenting with 'seeker services'. I am not aware of anywhere in Britain where large numbers of people are becoming Christians through it as yet, but it is early days. The movement has already done a great deal of good. It has brought home to many of us just what a 'turn-off' some of our church services can be to those who are not used to church culture. It has encouraged many to experiment with new approaches and with greater use of drama and music. Two new jargon words have entered the Christian vocabulary: 'seeker-targeted' referring to a service arranged almost wholly with unchurched people in mind; and 'seeker-friendly' describing a service which, while catering for the needs of the existing congregation, is trying to be as acceptable as possible to a new person coming in.

Old-style guest services, and also the weekly family service, which we have just considered, would count as 'seeker-friendly'. Many would hold that, to be 'seeker-targeted', a service should not put guests into the position of singing or saying anything they do no mean. There should therefore be little or no hymn singing. There should be almost no prayer. The 'guts of the service' should be a presentation using art forms such as music and drama, together with a well-presented sermon. We shall consider 2 examples in the case studies below.

The attempt to become more 'seeker-friendly' must surely be a priority for almost every British church. There can be no argument.

What is harder to forecast is how the 'seeker-targeted' service will evolve in British culture. One point which needs to be faced by churches wondering whether to opt for this approach is the need for a speaker gifted in communicating with non-Christians. Not all clergy are good at it! At least half the appeal of Willow Creek is their main speaker, Bill Hybels, who seems to have a particular gift in this area. How many British churches have such a speaker? On the other hand, new approaches may develop which are less speaker-dependent. The first case study below is one such example.

☐   'Nice 'n' Easy' was a Thursday evening service designed by Conisbrough Parish Church for people who were put off by the thought of clergy and Sunday church. There were no clergy present and few ordinary church members other than those leading the service. The style was really that of a pub sing-along. In addition to the singing, there were prayers for needs which people gave as they came in, a talk, and a drinks break in the middle. Initially, about 40 people came along, of all ages but with the majority middle aged and upwards. The service still continues, but to an extent it has been the victim of its own success. Many of the first 40 have become Christians and joined the church, so the service can no longer be described as mainly for outsiders in the way it once was.

☐   Southcourt Baptist Church is the only church I have come across which has turned one of its regular weekly services into a Willow Creek style 'seeker-service'. It takes place in the evening, and there are normally up to 200 people present. I attended one week and enjoyed it enormously. After one congregational song at the beginning we were treated to a presentation consisting of 3 songs from the front together with 2 dramas and a video of a mime artist on a large screen. There was also a helpful talk on dealing with anger, which was the overall theme. The service ended with the group singing quietly the song 'I'm Accepted, I'm Forgiven' before the blessing.

It must be incredibly demanding to produce that level of creative input every week, but the church was seeing some reward for its efforts. The service was attracting around 20 non-Christians and a trickle had started coming to faith.

The last 2 cases are clearly very different from each other, not least because of the nature of their fringe. The Conisbrough service has an Institutional fringe. Many of those who came would know church members, but they were not mainly brought by a friend. They were a group of people whom the church was in touch with in one way or another. The point for an Osmosis church is clear. A 'seeker service' will not work of its own accord. There must be an adequate fringe to invite. You start with the target group, and then decide what sort of service will be appropriate. The dynamic is similar to a church plant, even if the actual location is the church, or church hall as it was for Conisbrough.

The Southcourt Baptist service was drawing on the Personal fringe. A number of those who had started to come were husbands of women in the church. The service was succeeding well, but it was not plugging in to a large receptive population. Thus, as with nearly all British churches, there seemed little prospect of it 'taking off' like Willow Creek. (Growth in a Web church is critically dependent on such factors as the size of catchment area and the receptivity of the population. This is argued in more detail in chapter 12.)

Southcourt Baptist's was one of the most appealing services I have ever attended, but it was an extremely demanding one in terms of the creative input. Not every church would have the resources. It is interesting to compare the approach with that of the Alpha course (see p. 85), which is an alternative approach to 'seeker-targeting'. The Alpha course approach requires far less input because it is repeatable. The same talks are given every time!

Power and Praise

In many ways the Willow Creek phenomenon can be seen as a counter-tendency to a movement which gained much following in Britain in the 1980s, the 'power evangelism' movement. The visits to Britain of John Wimber, leader of the Vineyard network of churches, added many new adherents to an approach which was already popular in some Pentecostal and charismatic circles. The basic philosophy is that people become receptive to God when they see evidence of supernatural power. Furthermore, praise and worship truly emanating from the heart give God a channel to move in a meeting. Thus one of the most important ways of helping a church forward in evangelism is to encourage heartfelt worship and the use of the charismatic gifts, such as healing and the 'word of knowledge'. While Willow Creek are saying that non-Christians should not be expected to take part in worship, Wimber and other charismatics were saying the more worship the better! As non-Christians come into the service and experience the evident presence of God, they will open up to him.

How can we resolve this antithesis? To an extent the truth can lie on both sides of the same coin. It must be true that many enquiring visitors will be impressed by worship which they can see comes from the heart. On the other hand, some of the New Church leaders I spoke to have felt for some years that the evangelistic claims made for praise celebrations in the past were often unrealistic. Furthermore, handwaving and dancing may encourage some, but they can certainly turn off others! The truth is that the charismatic churches, including many of the New Churches, have been deeply influenced by Willow Creek. That is not to say they have now abandoned power evangelism. Rather, Willow Creek has encouraged such churches to work at removing the 'cringe factors'. Worship times are often shorter and the Christians are sometimes encouraged not to dance, for example, when visitors are present. Healing ministry and the use of spiritual gifts, though, are still considered important for evangelism.

We consider the issue of 'power evangelism' further in chapter 8.

8 Helping Enquirers

We now move to the bottom of the chart on p. 25. We have already referred to several approaches to Persuasion evangelism, and shall now consider them in a little more detail. There is no substantial research to be reported on in this chapter. The purpose is mainly descriptive, though I shall make some attempt at evaluation based on a mixture of personal judgement and some significant conversations during the research project.

Enquirers Groups

The first survey asked how many people had come to faith through enquirers' groups. If we include groups meeting in the person's home, the figure came to 282, or 27% of those who had become Christians.

Churches run a very wide variety of courses. Some use 'off the peg' materials produced by their denomination or a Christian organization. Others produce their own material. We cannot hope, here, to make any comparison between even the more popular courses, nearly all of which are very good. Our prime concern will be the 'link strategies', the ways in which people become involved in the groups. It may also be helpful, though, to consider some of the main characteristics of these courses.

First, where does the course start from? Some start from the enquirer, with an 'any questions?' approach: 'You ask the questions, and we will try to answer them.' Others start from the Bible, and are structured so that the most important features of Christian faith are all covered. This still gives the enquirer plenty of opportunities to ask questions. The underlying philosophy is really 'Let us tell you about Christianity. Then when you have heard about it, you will be in a position to form your own judgement.' I would describe this as the Christian 'basics' approach, as it is very like a 'basics' or nurture group, though with a different dynamic with non-Christians present.

Different types of material are available. The more structured courses usually rely on Bible study material of some form. Some leaders use video material, not necessarily every week. This may be provided as part of the course, for example the CPAS 'Basics' course. Other leaders use extracts from videos which they find helpful on particular weeks.

For example, one minister uses the crucifixion scene from Zeffirelli's *Jesus of Nazareth* when considering the cross.

The content of courses is remarkably similar, even across churchmanship. Issues such as whether there is a God, the person of Christ, and why he died are central for us all. One point of variation, however, is whether the course contains a charismatic emphasis. Some, such as 'Saints Alive', include an opportunity for members to be prayed with to be filled with the Holy Spirit, together with some teaching on spiritual gifts. Clearly, churches need to choose material that suits their own emphasis.

The length of the course is obviously important. If it is too short, enquirers may go away with their questions unanswered. If it is too long they will not be willing to attend! There is a trend at the moment for 'basics' courses to become longer. Many churches are recognizing that 6 weeks is insufficient time to give someone a grounding in Christian faith. The discipleship programme at Willow Creek lasts from one to two years, and, for example, adult catechumenate groups can last for up to 30 weeks. There is much to be said for this when the group are already committed, but in an enquirers' group we are dealing with wary fish! Some may not be prepared to commit themselves for more than 2 or 3 evenings. This type of group will usually be of the 'any questions' variety. A typical length for an enquirers' group might be 6 weeks, but some 'basics' groups, which also draw in enquirers, last up to 15 weeks.

One very important area where, in my opinion, some courses are lacking, is the handling of the challenge to commitment. Coming to faith is a process, but it also needs a point of crisis. In some cases this is covered liturgically through baptism or confirmation. Otherwise, though, it would normally be embarrassing to deal with it in the group. Some courses build in a personal interview towards the end of the course, and this can be a very helpful opportunity for such personal discussion. Some churches acknowledge the weakness of their small groups for handling personal commitment, and hold an evangelistic guest service at around the time the group finishes. This would not be appropriate, though, in every church. Different churches will wish to tackle the issue in different ways, but it needs thinking about lest we hold something rather like a diving class which never takes the members down to the pool for a dive!

The name of an enquirers' group is extremely important, and needs to take into account the perceptions of those who will join. Not everyone sees themself as an 'enquirer'. Many fringe folk consider themselves to be Christians, and it is only as the group progresses they realize there is more to it than they imagined. Some of the titles I have come across include 'Just Looking', 'Open to Question', 'School of Faith', 'Christian Basics', 'Confirmation Class', 'Adult Catechumenate' and 'Welcome Course'. One church which uses the last title is an Anglican church with a good fringe, where many new arrivals to the church do not have a clear personal faith. They are happy to join a 'welcome course', whereas they might feel threatened by a title which implied they were not Christians. In other churches, however, many men in particular would not wish to go to a group which might imply that they saw themselves already as Christians. In this case, a title such as 'Just Looking' would be more appropriate.

Who comes to enquirers' and 'basics' groups, and how are they invited? A high percentage of those who come, particularly in Osmosis-style churches, are invited by the minister or one of the church leaders. An unpublished study by Captain David Sanderson of the Church Army looking at 31 Christian 'basics' groups found that only 7 involved people from completely outside the church. Most of those who came were already Christians, or were part of the Institutional fringe. Surely this must be a weakness. Is there some way of adapting the enquirers' group approach to draw in friends of church members who may have little or no contact with the church?

One church which has attempted this is Christ Church, Bridlington, which has made available enquirers' group material of varying kinds for use by church members. At any one time, 2 or 3 of these groups are likely to be in progress. They will probably be quite small, with 2 or 3 members each, but at least it is an attempt to push the enquirers' groups out a little from the centre. Even at Bridlington, though, most of the groups are for those who already attend services, or are part of the church's community groups. Occasionally someone will arrange a group with 2 or 3 friends, say from college, but this is the exception rather than the rule. We shall see a dramatically different picture when we consider the HTB Alpha course below.

EVANGELISM EXPLOSION

Evangelism Explosion began in an evangelical Presbyterian church in Florida. I had always imagined it was as brash as its name! I knew that it involved asking people 2 important questions to help them face up to the challenge of whether they were really a Christian. The first question is: 'Have you come to the place in your life when you can say for certain that if you were to die tonight you would go to heaven?' The second is: 'Suppose you were to die and stand before God and he was to say to you, "Why should I let you into my heaven?" what would you say?' Readers will have differing attitudes to such an approach. Personally speaking, I accepted it in principle, but believed it would be far too instant and 'hard sell' for Britain.

I was wrong. Evangelism Explosion has been adapted to British culture.[1] If it ever was as I had imagined, it is not so now – at least, it need not be. There is always a danger of it being practised in an insensitive and confrontational way, but that is not how it is taught. The emphasis in EE now is on gentle building of relationships.

Why am I including Evangelism Explosion in this section? The fact is it is a form of Persuasion evangelism. It is really a bit like a 1-session enquirers' group in the home. Fringe contacts will be asked, often by the minister, whether they would mind a small team, usually of 3 people, coming to share their faith. If the contact is willing an appointment is made. The group have a relaxed evening together, during which team members share their personal experience of Christ. If the person wants to take it further, a second appointment is arranged. The enquirers' group goes on as long as the host wishes!

The benefits of EE go beyond the arranged visits. It is primarily a training in personal evangelism which should help Christians share their faith in many contexts. The current British training course lasts for 12 evenings, and involves practical experience in the form of home visits as well as 'classroom' learning. Trainees visit the homes of 'warm' contacts in pairs, each with a trainer who has completed the course previously. Several ministers have told me how valuable they have found this training personally.

EE's big advantage, as a form of Persuasion evangelism, is that it is extremely flexible. It can reach people, particularly from the Institutional fringe, that other approaches will not reach. Even EE, though, does need moderately warm contacts, and a lack of realism here can result in disappointment. One Anglican minister had tried it with all his funeral contacts from the past year, but it had not worked. They were not sufficiently warm. Others, though, had found it worked with a proportion of funeral contacts after they had been 'warmed up' by a number of pastoral visits first.

I have not met so widely divergent views in my research on any other topic as on EE. I have met ministers who claim it does not work. I have met others for whom it has transformed their church. Some have claimed it does not work in their particular culture, be it working class or middle class. Yet I have found examples of it working well in virtually every type of culture – in a large rural village, on a tough council estate, amongst Asians and in middle-class areas.

In my opinion, culture is not the prime issue. The key point is that EE takes considerable persistence to get started and to keep going. The use of the apprentice method, together with the need for warm contacts, places a limit on the numbers who can be trained at any one time. In practice it may take several years before a good proportion of the church are trained. The minister must, therefore, be very committed to it. All the ministers I spoke to who had used it effectively gave me the impression that personal evangelism was very important in their own gifting and motivation.

In practice, the experience of several churches I have spoken to is that the evangelistic results of EE coincide with the training courses. In many ways this works well. The need to find warm contacts for the training provides a powerful incentive for evangelism. Many churches, though, find it hard to maintain the momentum between courses.

A further point is that none of the churches I spoke to where EE was the key stimulus in producing real growth were very large. That is not to say that no large churches use it. Nor is it a criticism of EE, which is intended, anyway, to be used in conjunction with other forms of evangelism. My cautious suggestion, though, is that, while it can be used as a valuable means of training in any size of church, in the British context it best provides an overall motor for growth in a small or medium-sized church of up to, say, 150 people.

It is fair to say that most of the churches which use Evangelism Explosion are evangelical. Nevertheless, to my surprise, I have discovered Roman Catholic churches using a very similar approach. The EE training programme has been adapted into an 'evangelization course' by Steubenville Franciscan University, near Pittsburgh. They have kept the second question the same but the first one is now slightly more open ended: 'Suppose you were to meet Jesus today, and he asked you "Who do you say that I am?" what would you say?' I like that question. There are no wrong answers! Father Tom Kenny, parish priest at the English Martyrs church in Wakefield, for example, is using this course, and intending to draw people into the church's adult catechumenate (see below). Several other churches in Wakefield diocese are taking it up.

The motivational advantages of EE are considered, together with a case study, in chapter 11.

GOOD NEWS DOWN THE STREET

Good News Down the Street is a blend of Evangelism Explosion and a 'basics' group.[2] It originated when Michael Wooderson, an Anglican vicar, wanted something to take to people showing an interest in Christian faith in their homes. He was impressed by Evangelism Explosion, but felt it a bit too instant, and realized that it needed a great deal of training for the team. His solution was to write a 6-week 'basics' course and to produce it in such a way that members of his church could take it to people in their homes. Like Evangelism Explosion, he used teams of 3 people. The purpose of this was to provide the maximum training opportunity. Training was 'on the job'. Many people have expected that having 3 people on the team might be a problem, but this does not seem to be so. The pattern used by some churches is to use a team of 3 for a couple, but if a single person is enquiring they send a team of 2.

Good News Down the Street has been extremely effective. In the research slightly more people, 159, were brought to faith through Good

News Down the Street than through enquirers' groups, though the presence of Michael Wooderson's church in the sample could have biased the result!

One great advantage of Good News Down the Street is that it solves the problem of how to 'put the question' regarding Christian commitment. After the fifth session, the people doing the course are asked to think before next week whether they would like to become Christians. It is all very ordinary and unpressured. Most do, and the leaders say a simple prayer with them during the next session; but for those who do not, though there might be slight disappointment, there is no embarrassment. Usually it has been clear that they have remaining questions. It is much more relaxed than in a larger group. I have personal experience of Good News Down the Street, and it was a great joy to find people becoming Christians quite naturally, without my being involved in any way, except maybe in setting up the course.

Good News Down the Street can be adapted for individual church needs. Michael Wooderson encourages churches to write their own material. While his own course centred round a factual look at the Jesus of the Gospels, others have used different approaches. One church in a UPA area, for example, uses a version with an emphasis on healing ministry, while a Baptist church uses a course based on the 'Four Spiritual Laws'. The approach is completely flexible, though a surprising number of churches do still use Michael Wooderson's original course.

How should a church choose between Good News Down the Street and a 'basics' or enquirers' group? Both approaches are suitable to most cultures. Much depends on whether people like being in a group. Students and young single people, for example, will probably enjoy being in a group. They are not in the least bit shy about joining in a discussion, and will probably enjoy meeting the other people. Others might feel less confident. Personally, for an ordinary family church, I feel Good News Down the Street has many advantages. It is possible to work with both husband and wife, with no babysitting problems. It can get round difficulties such as shiftwork as the sessions can be arranged at the couple's convenience. It trains and motivates members of the congregation. We have already seen how it handles the tricky issue of the challenge to Christian commitment. Finally, it utilizes all 3 strands of the evangelistic Cord – prayer, teaching, and friendship. The members of the team should be able to keep in touch with and encourage those who have done the course, which the minister and helpers might not be able to do so well after an enquirers' group.

THE ADULT CATECHUMENATE

Receive the sign of the Cross on your ears,
That you may hear the voice of the Lord.

Receive the sign of the Cross on your eyes,
That you may see the glory of God.

Receive the sign of the Cross on your lips,
That you may respond to the Word of God.

Receive the sign of the Cross over your heart,
That Christ may dwell there by faith.

Receive the sign of the Cross on your shoulders,
That you may bear the gentle yoke of Christ.[3]

These moving words come from the Rite of Christian Initiation of Adults (RCIA) of the Roman Catholic church. Its modern roots go back to Vatican 2. Responding to the increasing number of converts wanting baptism as adults, particularly in the developing world, the Council decreed that the catechumenate of adults should be restored. 'Catechumenate' comes from a Greek word meaning to teach or instruct. In the first few centuries of Christianity, though not in the *very* earliest years, there was a lengthy period of catechesis for those who sought baptism. This could take several years, during which the catechumens were considered part of the family of the church though they were not yet baptized, and they could not yet take part in the eucharist.

The process is divided into four stages: the period of evangelization (or pre-catechumenate); the period of the catechumenate; the period of purification and enlightenment; and the period of post-baptismal catechesis or mystagogy. In layman's terms these stages could be described as an enquirers' course, a 'basics' course, a short devotional confirmation course, and finally, after the baptism and confirmation, a discipleship course during which moral and other issues relating to living out the faith are explored. Often this is tied to the church's year, with the period of evangelization starting in Advent, and the baptism and confirmation taking place at Easter.

Between each stage, those involved take part in a liturgy during the parish mass, in addition to other rites in the small group. One purpose of this is to ensure that the whole of the Christian community are involved in what is going on, praying, encouraging, and in some cases being more involved still. Ideally, every candidate should have a sponsor who also comes to the group and who will pray for the candidate and answer questions. This is in marked contrast to most enquirers' groups where other church members are usually unaware they are taking place!

While the rites are prescribed, the course material which is used is up to the discretion of the parish priest. Certain values are nearly always reflected in the approach. There is an emphasis on first 'telling your story', and of everyone being on a journey. 'Formation comes before information.'

The adult catechumenate is also used in many Anglican churches, particularly those in the catholic tradition.[4] As in the Roman church, there is a variety of material used in the group sessions. This need not be specific to the catechumenate. For example, some groups use Good News Down the Street during the pre-catechumenate stage.

What are we to make of the catechumenate approach? It has four fairly obvious strengths. First, it is thorough, giving plenty of time to the vital task of conversion. The reader will doubtless be aware that catholics use the term in a process sense, referring to a gradual change of heart and mind over a period of time. Second, through use of the rites, and also of the different emphases of the four stages, it combines the intellectual and devotional aspects of the spiritual search better than an ordinary enquirers' group. Third, it uses all three strands of the evangelistic Cord in helping people forward: prayer, teaching, and fellowship, aided by the use of the sponsors. Fourth, it works! The churches I have spoken to have been enthusiastic. Lives have been changed by the groups, and have sometimes been an inspiration and challenge to others in the church.

Nevertheless, the catechumenate has its critics. The biggest charge is that it is too 'churchy'. The language and style of the catechumenate seems a mile away from modern secular people. Even though some churches use modern language and names such as 'Journey into Life' groups, some of the traditional flavour, it is argued, remains. This may even be an advantage for some, but probably not for the completely unchurched. Also, the length of the course and the need to stand publicly in church for the rites can make it sound rather daunting for some enquirers.

A second criticism is that it is inflexible. Certainly, the fact that it can only take place once a year must mean it is not available at the right time for some enquirers. In theory some kind of pre-catechumenate could be run several times a year, though I am not aware of it happening in practice.

The most objective assessment of the effectiveness of the catechumenate in drawing people in would be a comparison of the numbers who take part, as compared with 'basics' or enquirers' groups. I have no such clear evidence. Nevertheless, 20 is an exceptional RCIA group in a British Roman Catholic church, and, bearing in mind that many Catholic churches have more than 500 adults, and that groups run only once a year, this does not seem very large. The biggest Anglican groups seem mainly to contain people who have made at least some kind of commitment through other forms of evangelism.[5] This does, at least, give some credence to the criticisms of those who feel the catechumenate is too 'churchy' for real outsiders. Maybe the catechumenate is best compared against 'basics' groups, against which it scores well, though being less flexible.

What can evangelicals, in particular, learn from the catechumenate? The biggest challenge must be the use of the public rites. Some will argue that there is no scriptural basis for the use of any rite for becoming a Christian other than baptism. True. Yet those who dwell in glass-houses should not throw stones, particularly if they are Anglican evangelicals like me! We happily live with confirmation, even though most of us accept its theological justification is thin in the extreme. What is more, the standard evangelical way of becoming a Christian is really very new indeed. We advise people to 'say a prayer to ask Jesus to come in as your personal Lord and Saviour'. There is, of course, no example of anyone doing any such thing in Scripture! We justify it on the grounds of expediency. Yet baptism, the New Testament way of becoming a Christian, was usually public, and was originally carried out without delay. If we are to delay baptism or confirmation for reasons of expediency, some kind of public testimony and prayer at an early stage must surely be in accord with the scriptural approach. The use of the rites seems to me to achieve this well. At least it makes it clear that becoming a Christian is not solely a transaction between the individual and God, but is part of joining his Church.

'I am speaking as a fool', to quote St Paul. I have no clear proposals. I am not suggesting that evangelicals should take on board the catechu-menate lock, stock, and barrel. Nevertheless, surely there is something to learn from the way catholics are bringing adult conversion into the midst of the fellowship through use of the public rites.

THE HTB ALPHA COURSE

The Alpha Course only came on to the public stage in May 1993 when Holy Trinity, Brompton attracted about 500 church leaders to a conference in London with the news that 450 people had attended their latest 'basics' course, more than half of them non-churchgoers![6] The course began 15 years ago in a curate's flat after a church mission. It grew steadily. In the early years, most of those who attended were new Christians. As time went on, the percentage of enquirers grew, and many of those who became Christians during the course invited their friends to the next one.

How does an Alpha Course work? It runs for 10 evenings, once a week, and there is a weekend away on the Holy Spirit as well. Each evening starts with a meal, and great pains are taken to ensure that unchurched people feel at ease. After the meal there is a time of worship, perhaps surprisingly, but it is sufficiently well-led to turn more on than off! Nicky Gumbel, the course leader, then gives a talk lasting about half an hour on standard Christian 'basics' topics. Afterwards people split into small groups. There were 140 leaders of these groups at a recent Alpha Course, and these were included in my estimate of 450 attending.

Why has the course been so successful? The evenings are well run, and Nicky is a gifted speaker. Nevertheless, this hardly explains the extraordinary difference between the results at HTB and most other churches. Nicky Gumbel believes that the emphasis on the Holy Spirit, particularly the weekend away, is a key factor. The course has a strongly charismatic emphasis, and during the weekend there is a time of asking the Holy Spirit to come and 'touch' the participants. The results are usually dramatic. In a quite different way from the adult catechumenate, the course combines intellectual enquiry with a more directly spiritual approach. Nicky believes that the infilling of the Holy Spirit provides a powerful motivation for many attenders to bring their friends. At the end of each course there is an Alpha supper to which friends are invited, and recently these have been packed full with 1,000 people attending!

I do not doubt this explanation in part. It has to be said that at *most* 'basics' courses a good percentage of the enquirers who attend will become Christians. As a convinced charismatic myself I fully accept that the 'power evangelism' approach will unlock some extra doors. In the next section we see how this applies particularly with certain types of enquirer. Does this, though, fully explain the phenomenal growth?

It needs to be understood that Holy Trinity, Brompton, is a Web church. So are nearly all the very large churches in Britain. What HTB has done is to combine a 'basics' group with a powerful Web dynamic. Whereas, as we saw, in most 'basics' groups, most of those who attend are invited by the minister or some other leader, at the Alpha Course almost no one is invited in this way. They are invited by their friends.

What is more, HTB is working effectively amongst a receptive population, young professionals in West London. It is true that not everyone who attends Alpha is in this age group. For example, many parents come. Nevertheless, I would need some convincing that the young professional network is not the tree from which the other branches grow. It is a classic case of those who become Christians having enough friends to sustain the growth. The fire generates enough heat to maintain the blaze.

There is another point. The Alpha Course provides an effective link strategy between Proclamation and Persuasion. The proclamation takes place in the first part of the evening, and the persuasion or 'discussion' happens in the small groups. Let us compare this with what happens at a guest service. If somebody is challenged by a sermon, it is then necessary to arrange for them to attend a suitable enquirers' group. There may be a time delay before the next group starts. People will inevitably be lost on the way. There is no such difficulty with Alpha.

In some respects the Alpha Course resembles a British enculteration of the Willow Creek seeker service. The occasion is 'seeker-targeted'. This is assisted by many of those present being part of a homogeneous group, young professionals. Many of the testimonies of those converted at Alpha start with the person saying how amazed they were, when they arrived at the hall, that the people looked normal! Part of this, surely, is that they are the kind of people they would normally socialize with.

How appropriate is the Alpha Course to the majority of churches? The growth in such courses has been remarkable. Within a year of the original conference, at the time of writing, 400 courses are running. Most, inevitably, are quite small, but it is early days. The essential thing to bear in mind is that the Alpha Course is really a 'basics' group adapted to a larger attendance than small group or living-room size. The format is a talk followed by discussion in smaller groups. It is a great deal of work for the minister or course leader to prepare a talk each week if there will only be 4 or 5 people present. The dynamics also do not work so well then. Nicky Gumbel suggests that 25 to 30 is the ideal size for an Alpha Course. For very small groups he recommends using a tape or video, but in many respects this is really more like an ordinary 'basics' group. I have come across a number of churches using the Alpha Course in my research, and several of those which have found it most valuable have been quite large churches which have a history of running 'basics' groups anyway, and have used the Alpha approach to raise the profile, and draw more people in.

Are there lessons to be learned for smaller Osmosis-style churches, whether or not they use the excellent Alpha materials? In my opinion, the biggest lesson is the need to tap into such Web dynamics as may exist. Even in Osmosis churches, people have friends! There is no reason why any 'basics' or enquirers' group which has 'jelled' should not end with a social occasion of some sort to which friends could be invited. There may be a talk, or course members may simply explain informally how helpful they have found it. It should generate at least some interest for the next group. Some courses, such as 'Saints Alive', recommend this approach already. My experience, not surprisingly, is that it works best in churches where there is already something of a Web dynamic.

One of the most important lessons to be learned from Alpha, however, must surely be for evangelism amongst receptive populations. For Web churches it is the most natural approach, and the potential is truly enormous. Paul Simmons of CPAS, in a book on reaching the unchurched, suggested that our best evangelists should base themselves in centres of population where they could teach week by week at seeker services.[7] I should like to suggest, as an alternative, running Alpha courses! They are sharper. Consider the potential amongst students and teenagers. The 'feel' of the evening would need to be geared to local culture. There might, for example, be drama and a different type of music.[8] Why should not such occasions acquire a greater buzz even than at HTB? Young people would bring their friends in droves.

Power Evangelism

We have now referred to 'power evangelism' twice: in the last section on the Alpha Course, and also in chapter 7 looking at church services. We cannot completely avoid a contentious question, 'Does it actually work?' Despite enthusiastic claims, some research would suggest not. In the CTE Research, for example, few, even from the charismatic churches, mentioned healing or the gifts of the Spirit as being significant in their faith journey.[9] In support of this view, it is not hard to find churches which are experiencing much encouragement in terms of spiritual gifts and even healing, but where few people are becoming Christians.

Against this, there are some churches where many come to faith as a result of power ministry. We have already considered Holy Trinity, Brompton, where, in the judgement of the leaders, an emphasis on the Holy Spirit has tipped the balance for many enquirers. In a very different social context is St John's, Abbey Hulton, an Anglican church serving a deprived UPA parish near Stoke-on-Trent. Brian Nash, team vicar till 1992, estimated that for 50 people coming to faith over a 6-year period, prayer ministry was involved in virtually every case. Part of the reason is that the church had developed its own charismatic version of Good News Down the Street, and this itself involved prayer and laying on of hands.[10] It is worth noting that here, as at HTB, the influence was felt at the Persuasion end of the evangelization process.

My own tentative conclusion is that it is rare, in the British context, for an emphasis on healing and charismatic ministry to produce substantial evangelistic fruit on its own. Nevertheless, where the social and spiritual processes are such that evangelism is already happening, an emphasis on these areas can certainly increase the flow. There is also some evidence that power ministry can be particularly important at certain times and amongst certain cultural groups. Stuart Murray, one of the founders of the Tower Hamlets Christian Fellowship, a vibrant multiracial church in a tough area of East London, gave me some interesting information. During the 12 years he was there, most people became Christians through friendship evangelism. During one exceptional 5-month period, however, there was a time of explosive evangelism. It was like a mini revival. In that time many became Christians through healing and the use of spiritual gifts in the services. Furthermore, of the 10 or so people from Muslim or Sikh backgrounds who became Christians while he was there, *all* of them did so because of a dream, or vision or healing.

Nicky Gumbel also gives support for the idea that certain groups may be particularly responsive to power ministry. His experience of the Alpha Course has been that scientists are less helped by it than artists, whereas it can be vital for those who have been involved with the New Age.[11]

A number of people have suggested to me that power evangelism can be particularly effective in UPA areas (as at Abbey Hulton). There seem to be three reasons for this: as a style of ministry it is quite physical and warm and appeals to those in need; it is not too cerebral – anyone can be involved; and there are often many with occult and other problems needing deliverance ministry in the inner city. One minister of a Liverpool council estate church estimated that he acquired a third of his congregation through helping them get free from the occult.

This is a major area of debate on which the reader may already hold a committed position theologically. My aim is simply to share one or two relevant pieces of information from the research.

Choosing an Approach

We have considered 5 different methods for helping enquirers: enquirers' groups, Evangelism Explosion, *Good News Down the Street*, the adult catechumenate, and the Alpha Course. How should we decide between them? Let us summarize the strengths and possible difficulties for each.

ENQUIRERS' GROUPS

Strengths
- Good standard approach, particularly for those who feel confident in a group
- Can cope with open-ended 'any questions?' approach

Possible Difficulties
- Inflexible for those on shifts or needing baby sitters
- It can be difficult to handle the challenge to commitment in a group

Optimum size of group: 6 to 15

EVANGELISM EXPLOSION

Strengths
- Extremely flexible. Will reach homes that other approaches will not reach
- Mobilizes prayer and involves congregation
- Good personal links for follow-up
- Valuable training in its own right

Possible Difficulties
- Needs much persistence to launch and sustain
- Needs good supply of warm contacts (so does every approach, but training course highlights the fact with EE)
- May not appeal to non-evangelicals

Optimum size of group: 1 or 2 plus team

GOOD NEWS DOWN THE STREET

Strengths
- Very flexible
- Easy to launch
- Mobilizes prayer and involves congregation
- Good personal links for follow-up

Possible Difficulties
- May need supplementing by 'basics' course if large number of enquirers at once – for example, after a mission

Optimum size of group: 1 or 2 plus team, though larger group possible

ADULT CATECHUMENATE

Strengths
- Very thorough, and operates on several levels
- Mobilizes prayer, and involves the congregation through use of sponsors and the public rites
- Good links for follow-up

Weaknesses
- Can appear 'churchy' to some types of enquirer
- Somewhat inflexible – for example, can only run once a year

Optimum size of group: 6 plus

ALPHA COURSE

Strengths
- The only approach which majors on attracting the Personal fringe. Enormous potential for growth in receptive population
- Can cater for large numbers

Possible Difficulties
- Needs adequate sized group to get started, and people with friends to bring
- Needs reasonably gifted speaker for non-Christians, unless tape or video is used

Optimum size of group: Best 20 plus, though can be used for smaller group

It will be seen that, for many churches, the number of enquirers will go some way to determining the most suitable approach. The reader will decide on the basis of local conditions. Let us be clear, though, we are comparing good with good. All the forms of Persuasion evangelism have brought great blessing. The most important thing is that some viable approach is being used to help those who are seriously interested in Christian faith.

Cell Groups

At the finish of this chapter I simply note that there is an alternative approach to Persuasion evangelism from any of the above. That is to incorporate enquirers straight into the home groups or 'cells' of the church, without any interim step such as an enquirers' group. The potential is enormous in theory, but I have not found any cases of it working properly in Britain.

We shall look at this option briefly in chapter 11. I mention it here simply to complete the picture of the options available for Persuasion evangelism.

9 Proclamation Evangelism and Special Events

There is a verse in the book of Jeremiah which speaks of the Word of God as fire and 'like a hammer that breaks a rock in pieces'.[1] That is how some Christians think of Proclamation evangelism. The preacher stands, Bible in hand, in a bar. There is drink and worldliness everywhere, and the crowd mock. Suddenly there is a cry. The biggest man present hits the deck and starts to cry out in repentance. The Word of God has cracked open his heart!

I do not deny that the Word of God has power to reach people's hearts. Usually, though, it is a gradual process. The reader will have noticed that the underlying model in the bar incident was crisis evangelism. The man had been bought from −10 to zero on the Engel scale in one bound, or should I say crash?

How effective are evangelistic events, by which I mean meals and other occasions at which there is an evangelistic talk? If the results of the first survey can be taken at face value, they are extraordinarily ineffective. Out of roughly 1,000 new Christians, only 2 had been significantly influenced by evangelistic events run by their own church (appendix 2, table A7). Admittedly, that estimate may be artificially low. The 2 churches which appeared to have run the most effective events did not complete the relevant question in the survey. Nevertheless, the CTE Research found that only 4% of new Christians said an evangelistic event, including Billy Graham and other such city-wide rallies, had been a main factor in their coming to faith, while 13% said it had been a supporting factor.[2]

In contrast to this, in question 8 of the first survey, ministers rated the effectiveness of their evangelistic events as being at least tolerable. Fifty percent saw them as being 'adequate' or 'good', as against 54% for adult guest services, 64% for guest family services, and 57% for social events with no talk (see appendix 2, table A4). We need to consider the reason for this apparent divergence. It may, in part, be due to over-optimism by ministers concerning the value of evangelistic events. I believe, though, there is an additional explanation.

The relatively high estimate of the evangelistic impact of social occasions with no talk is interesting, and we shall consider it further below. It partly explains the small number of people for whom special events are key factors in their becoming Christians. Evangelistic events are to do with process rather than crisis. We may think of them as to do with Proclamation, but they are as much to do with Presence. Certainly, the speaker's message is important, but something more complex is going on. Attitudes are being changed and prejudices broken down. Relationships are being made, and people are discovering that Christians are not so weird after all. Those who come are weighing up whether becoming a Christian is a viable option for them.

Seen in this light, it is not surprising that few see such events as the *main influence* in their becoming a Christian. That is more likely to be the friend who brought them, the minister, or church services when they start to attend. Nevertheless, the events can be a helpful influence on the way. This is precisely what the CTE Research said. Only 4% considered it a main influence, but 13% said it was a supporting factor.

Proclamation Evangelism Survey

I should like now to give the results of a survey I sent to 30 members of the Fellowship for Parish Evangelism, a grouping of Anglicans involved in evangelism in different ways. 24 forms were returned, a marvellous response rate of 80%. I sent the forms to those whom I knew were not only experienced evangelists, but thought very seriously about strategy as well. They include some of Britain's best known evangelists as well as a number of men who have experience both as travelling evangelists and as church-based ministers. I am grateful to such busy people for returning their forms.

The respondents were asked to rate the effectiveness of different types of Proclamation evangelism, as listed in table 5, for different types of community and church scene. Admittedly, the latter are over-simplified, and do not represent every type of area. I originally ran a pilot survey with more types of community, and also more types of evangelism, but the extra categories yielded almost no extra information. I decided to keep it simple. The categories of community and church scene were as follows:

A.   Inner City Council Estate
UPA estate, high level of deprivation. Minimal church attendance, even at major festivals. 80% unemployment.

B.   City Centre
Eclectic church. Many students and young professionals from 3-mile radius.

C.   Rural Village
500 people. Strong sense of community.

D. Middle-Class Outer Suburb

Large fringe: for example, high level of attendance at major festivals, particularly Christmas.

Respondents were asked to rate the types of evangelism from 1 to 5, where 5 meant very effective and 1 meant useless. They were to assume that the style of events – for example, the music and food – were as well-suited as possible to each culture. They were asked to respond only to those items for which they had experience, but many were in fact able to complete all the boxes. The results of the survey are summarized in table 5. There was considerable agreement for most items, but the asterisks indicate those areas where there was wide disagreement, with a mean deviation from the average score of more than 0.8.

	UPA A	City Centre B	Rural C	Suburb D	General Value for Men
Sunday Services[1]					
Guest services with evangelistic appeal	2.3*	3.9	3.1	3.6	2.8
Low-key seeker services	2.7	3.5	2.6	3.8	3.4*
Main festivals	3.0	3.1	4.0	3.8	2.9
Family services	3.3	2.6	3.5	3.8	2.5
Home Events					
Supper parties[2]	2.2*	3.7	3.6	3.9	3.4
Video evenings	3.4	2.9	3.0	2.9*	2.7
Social events with speaker					
Pub	3.8	3.5	3.8*	3.7	4.4
Sport events with speaker	3.3*	3.3*	3.2	4.0	4.5
Breakfast/dinner in hotel	1.8	3.7	3.5	4.2	4.4
Meal in church hall	2.9*	2.9	3.9	3.4	3..0

Table 5   Evangelism Effectiveness of Proclamation Events

Notes   1 Services geared to outsiders at which the gospel is preached, though where appropriate in a low-key way, not necessarily with an appeal
    2 Anything from coffee and cake to main meal

It is interesting to note the 'best bets' in each type of area: a pub evening on the UPA Estate; a guest service in the city centre church; a main festival service, targeted towards outsiders, in the rural area; and a dinner in a hotel (some said breakfasts were not preferred) in the outer suburb. It was notable that the best locations for men were considered to be neither the church, nor the home, but some neutral venue such as a pub or a hotel for larger group events.

It is not the place of this book to give detailed advice on any of the above approaches to evangelism. I shall limit myself to one or two comments on each main approach.

HOME EVENTS

Home events were a main factor for 23 people becoming Christians in the first survey (appendix 2, table A7). This is more than for larger events (2 people), but it is still only 2%.

In the right context, 'supper parties' will pack in more non-Christians to hear the gospel message than any other approach. That is because they gain the greatest involvement and commitment from the congregation. At each supper party, there should normally be around 6 visitors, in addition to team members who may 'tell their story' and the hosts who will provide the food. This multiplies up dramatically. When I was in Leicester, for example, in one mission we had 50 supper parties, which involved 300 non-Christians. We would never have attracted that number with larger group events.

One has to be realistic, though. Only a very small percentage of those who come to the home events will ever make it to a church service. The supper parties provide an excellent atmosphere for informal discussion, but they really are 'throwing the net out' quite wide. It is fairly obvious that they are most appropriate for a church with a good Personal fringe.

The normal context for supper parties is a visit from another church with a 'faith sharing' team – ordinary Christians who speak briefly about their faith as a prelude to discussion. Naturally, the team has to be booked in advanced. The mistake I have sometimes made is twisting the congregation's arms too hard to hold the suppers. The result has been that people with few friends to invite have valiantly organized a meal, inviting neighbours and acquaintances whom they have never previously had in their home. Infuriatingly, these people are too shy to say 'no', and say they will come; then, on the day, they do not turn up! This can be disheartening for the hosts, and can put them off trying anything like it again.

Many of the respondents to the Proclamation survey rated supper parties as only 1 or 2 in the UPA area, but this was balanced by a few who gave them 4 provided it was tea and cake as opposed to a full meal. It is impossible to generalize. The number of cultural variations are legion. Nevertheless, if you are dealing with people with small rooms, who are not used to inviting people into their homes, and the people being invited are not used to coming, you are pushing your luck! I think, now, I would always try one or two on an experimental basis before organizing a major mission around supper parties.

Video evenings are really an alternative to supper parties, and can be more acceptable to people in working-class areas, particularly if they do not know the host very well. This is reflected in the score of 3.4 for the UPA area. Watching a video is a fairly normal thing to do, and does not feel threatening. There are 2 approaches. One is to show a full-length film such as *Chariots of Fire*, and the other is to show a half-hour Christian testimony video. I prefer the latter, because it allows more time for discussion, though it obviously depends on who is being invited. There is a wide range of excellent testimony videos available, suitable for different cultures and churchmanships.

The difficulty about video evenings is that it is hard to get very many of them off the ground. If you arrange a faith sharing team it provides an impetus for holding, say, 12 supper parties over a weekend. It is harder to get the same head of steam for videos, particularly if you only have 2 or 3 viable ones to use.

LARGE GROUP EVENTS

I shall say little on these, although we shall be considering them further in the next chapter on men's evangelism. Let us consider their role as alternatives, on the one hand, to supper parties and home events, and on the other hand to guest and seeker services.

You are planning a weekend of Proclamation evangelism. Which is the preferable approach? Should you hold a series of small home meetings, or one large event in the hall or elsewhere? The best advice I have had from experienced evangelists is that it is simply a question of 'horses for courses'. Some people will prefer the anonymity of a larger event, while others will respond better to a personal invitation to someone's home. The small event will give an opportunity for people to 'get things off their chest', and for some this can be extremely important. Others, though, will find the home event threatening, and will prefer the anonymity of a larger group.

The second factor is the availability of a suitable meeting place. If there is a pub or club of some sort where local people naturally meet, that is obviously an ideal location. Some church halls, too, are better than others. We work with what is available.

One approach which combines some of the benefits of small and large group events is used by, and I think was invented by, the evangelist Ian Knox. This is a version of a progressive supper called 'Come to the Centre'. Church members invite friends and neighbours to the first course in their homes, and then at around 9 p.m., say, everyone gathers at a central venue for desserts and a talk. Each host takes their own dessert to the hall in advance, and it is quite impressive seeing them all set out! On one occasion when I did this we had a small jazz band playing at the hall, which added to the atmosphere. I have also used it with a visiting drama group. It is an excellent approach, making use of the 'pulling power' of supper parties, without the difficulty of people feeling they need to invite a large group. Even one couple will be enough, whereas at a supper party you really need at least 10 for people not to feel threatened.

Another strategic question to be faced is the emphasis to put on large group evangelistic events as against special services in church. Several evangelists made the point on their survey replies that the events draw in bigger numbers. There may be one or two exceptions to this. Large city centre Web churches can get big numbers for guest services. Carol services are another obvious exception. Generally though the events pull in more people. This was brought home to me during a mission at St Mary of Bethany Church in Woking recently with the evangelist Barry Kissell. We had good numbers all week, with about 200 visitors coming to a mixture of small and large group events. On Saturday evening, for example, 50 came for a glass of wine followed by some drama and a talk. At the Sunday morning guest service, though, which was intended as the climax to the mission, we only had 25 non-Christians present.

The point I wish to make is that many evening events are not so different from a seeker service. There is usually a singer, some drama and a talk. The only difference is that in a seeker service you probably sing one or two hymns, while at the event you are more likely to have some refreshment, which need not be very great. 'A rose by any other name!' I am sure this may vary from church to church, but I am coming to the view that in many cases we should avoid the term 'service'!

GUEST SERVICES

Several evangelists have made the point that guest services are no longer as effective as they once were. I am referring here to the kind of approach where friends are brought along to hear a gifted speaker in the hope that they will respond to a gospel challenge. As the level of knowledge about Christian faith has declined in our country, particularly amongst young people, most simply do not have the background to respond in this way. Even coupled with an offer to join an enquirers' group, such services are still not appropriate for many friends and contacts. The average number of guests at such services in the first survey, if baptismal services are excluded, was 12; and that was for those churches (one in three) which were enthusiastic enough about guest services to hold them. The main exceptions to this general rule are city centre churches and those which still have a good fringe. The highest score for guest services in the Proclamation Survey was from the student-oriented city centre church, with 3.9. This certainly accords with my experience. Out of the 189 people in the first survey who became Christians through a guest service, 147 were from one church – Gerrard Street Baptist Church in

Aberdeen – a city centre Web church with many students. This church holds around 6 such services a year. They are baptism services, and there are usually around 50 adult visitors at each.

The highest score of all for services was for a main festival in a rural area, scoring 4.0. Main festivals, of course, are the best time to hold guest services in any community with a degree of 'folk religion'. Chris Edmondson, who was previously Advisor for Evangelism in Carlisle Anglican diocese, a mainly rural area, made the point to me that you should sometimes even invent special Sundays in this kind of area: 'Plough Sunday', 'Rogation Sunday', these are the kind of times when country folk will come to their parish church!

Seeker services, main festivals, and family services all scored highly in the outer suburb, with a score of 3.8 in table 5. This makes complete sense, as the suburban church in the survey had been defined as having a large fringe.

Does all this mean that there is no role for guest services in most churches unless they have a large fringe? The answer, probably, is that they do still have a role if used sparingly. Several respondents made the point that I was combining two questions in one. Which events will attract visitors? And which will yield the greatest spiritual response? The respondents to the survey had little doubt that a service in church has a better atmosphere than an event for making a direct challenge to commitment.

MOTIVATING THE CONGREGATION

In several responses to the Proclamation survey from travelling evangelists there were comments which felt like something of a *cri de coeur*. 'Prayer, fasting, bringing' was Dan Cozens' comment. 'Prayer, preparation, bringing' was the comment from J. John. How can we motivate the Christians?

Some of the congregation, on the other hand, might put it differently: 'I have almost no one to invite; and the few people I do know locally would not come to the kind of events on offer.'

Which is the real problem? Are the congregation under-motivated, or is it really very hard bringing people to Christian occasions? One church, after very poor attendance at guest services, asked the congregation to complete a survey explaining why they had not brought people. They could give any number of reasons. The commonest are shown in table 6.

How do we motivate the 43% who *admitted* that inertia is the problem? One Anglican vicar, previously a church-based evangelist, tried several approaches. First he ran a friendship evangelism course, to train people in evangelism and give them confidence to invite friends to meetings. Very few came on the course. He then tried guilt! It still did not work.

Inertia. The problem is me!	43%
No one to invite	41%
Aspects of service off-putting	29%
Very idea of a service a 'turn-off'	24%
Need to have heard speaker in advance	19%

Table 6   Reasons for not Bringing Guests

Since then he has majored on building confidence as the only effective approach, running quality events consistently over a period of time until the congregation slowly get the message that it will be OK to invite their friends.

Some of the New Churches have a higher expectation of their congregations.

☐ The Aylsham Tabernacle Community Church in Norwich has grown from 70 to 250 in 4½ years, as well as planting a daughter church. Grantley Watkins is their full-time elder for evangelism, and he runs a course on friendship evangelism. It includes pastoral issues, such as caring for the sick and bereaved, as well as teaching on such things as being a good neighbour, being available, and how to 'lead someone to Christ'. *All* church members have been through this course, and their home-group leaders, with Grantley's assistance, follow them up and encourage where appropriate. There is, in effect, a covenant between the church leaders and the members: 'We provide opportunities for you to bring people, you cultivate a lifestyle of building friendships.'

☐ The Kingsland Church on the Byker estate, a UPA area in Newcastle, like Aylsham Tabernacle, is part of the New Frontiers network of churches. Lex Loizides is the full-time evangelist. His philosophy is very similar to Grantley's, even though working in a very different type of area. He believes there are 2 keys to an effective strategy of evangelization.

The first is motivating the congregation. To do this, they have to be convinced that evangelism can work. Much of this is done by personal example. For example, two-thirds of the congregation now have their own personal tract to give to friends, an idea initiated by Lex. I now have one too! There is also a slot in every prayer meeting to pray for the coming evangelistic events. They have prayer targets. They pray for the number of *guests* and that they will respond and join an enquirers' group.

The second key is that there must be a coherent strategy of evangelism using a mixture of approaches from advertising to mums and toddlers events to evangelistic meals, firework parties, and so on. The people contacted in these ways are encouraged to come to guest services, and, when they are seriously interested, to join the church's enquirers' course.[3]

Grantley and Lex are, in effect, using a two-pronged approach: motivating the congregation, and providing events to appeal to a wide cross-section of people at different points in their faith journey. We consider the role of the full-time evangelist in motivating a congregation for evangelism in chapter 11. In the meantime, let us consider something a little more 'soft sell'.

The Role of Social Events

Malcolm Potter is the Baptist missioner for Essex. His job is helping the Baptist churches in his region in evangelism. His approach is based on three principles he believes he has discovered:

1. If a friend or relative will come to 3 *quality* social events in a row, they will start coming to church.
2. If they come to church for 3 months, they will be willing to join an enquirers' group.
3. Of those who join an enquirers' group, a very high percentage become Christians and continue in the faith.

I am sure Malcolm would be the first to agree that there must be variations with culture and style of church. Nevertheless, I found his 3 points struck a chord. He is essentially putting forward the philosophy of a Stepping-Stones church, and saying that he has seen it work in many cases.

I have only recently come to see the evangelistic importance of social events. In the analysis of the first survey (appendix 2, table A4), it is interesting to see that there are more social events than directly evangelistic ones, and the ministers find them equally effective. It has been said that for most people cultural and social factors are greater barriers to them becoming Christians than intellectual or theological ones. If the talk in an evangelistic event is geared to help the latter problem, the rest of the event may be geared to the former. There is an old saying that Christianity is caught rather than taught. I can believe this. Once somebody has got to know some Christians who seem to have something in their lives that he or she lacks, the intellectual problems can usually be sorted out. Many of the church leaders I have spoken to have hinted at this in different ways. Steve Clifford, a leader in the Cobham Church in the Pioneer network of churches, said that one of the best events he could remember was a New Year's party. There was almost nothing 'religious' about it, though at midnight everyone raised their glasses and thanked God for a new year. The point was that it was a really well-run party, and it blew away many preconceptions. It did more than many sermons.

How are we to organize consistent, well-run social events? Will it not stretch the resources of many churches? Malcolm Potter's solution is that you should start with what the individual organizations are already planning, and upgrade it. If the youth group are going swimming, invite the toddler group mums and their husbands too, as well as other organizations. Then have snacks and a sing-along with a testimony back in the hall.

No one is suggesting that organizations should not have their own events. The church as a whole, though, needs one quality social event each month. Useful ideas, mostly gleaned from Stepping-Stone churches in the surveys have included: a quiz with good food and a confident quizmaster; a barn dance; a bonfire party; a family fun night; a carol concert in a pub; an alternative halloween party; and a Christian cabaret evening.

Another approach is having small group events organized by the home groups. They seem to be growing increasingly popular as home groups change their style. They need not be very hard to organize. They might be a barbecue in the garden, or simply playing a game of Trivial Pursuit. They are very valuable in certain circumstances. We saw in chapter 6 how Ichthus Fellowship, Deptford Park have used them. They are certainly no trouble to the church leadership to organize, as it is all delegated out to the home groups! Nevertheless, there are only certain people who can be invited. Non-Christian spouses will find it natural enough to join their other half for a home group barbecue or meal. Other friends, though, will often feel more relaxed going to a large group event.

Church Missions

What is the purpose of church missions? In the past they have often epitomized all that was wrong with our evangelism. It used to be said of evangelical churches, in particular, that they would hold a mission every 3 years, and then sit back and wait for the next one. That may have worked once, when there was more partial faith around in the community, but it certainly will not work now. Our evangelism, as we have seen, must be more process-oriented, and presumably people will be led into full Christian commitment as and when they are ready for it. In a healthy church, there should be no great fringe ready to be reaped when the visiting evangelist arrives. Is not the very idea of a mission now redundant?

I have not researched this, so I can only give my own views which may be no more informed than the reader's. In my opinion church missions do still have a role. Just as in long-distance running or rowing there will be times when it is appropriate to sprint or increase the stroke rate, so a church will benefit from the concentration of prayer and evangelistic thrust that comes from a mission. It should be a source of new ideas for the future, and new vision and encouragement will be gained, hopefully, from the missioner. Nevertheless, a church which is engaging in effective evangelism throughout the year may see less immediate 'fruit' from a mission than in years back when all the reaping was left to a visiting evangelist.

Does this not suggest, though, that we should be reconsidering the role of visiting evangelists? Is it appropriate that we still employ them, simply as reapers, when our aim is to be doing more of that ourselves?

☐   The Catholic Missionary Society, based in North West London, consists of a community of both ordained and lay people. They conduct missions in Roman Catholic churches throughout Britain, and in each case they maintain contact with the church for a period of about 18 months.

About a year before the mission, a member of CMS meets with the parish team consisting of the clergy and other key leaders to discuss the CMS strategy. If appropriate, dates are fixed for the mission. There is then a 'period of formation' at 3 levels.

First, the parish team attends a 2-day course at CMS, during which they think through the vision for the parish, and the necessary steps for attaining that vision.

Second, the parish team are asked to gather together a mission team consisting of 10 to 12 people. These are not to be the 'busy bees' who already do all the parish work. After meeting with the missioner, this group takes part in a series of 6 discussions using materials provided by CMS. The aim is that they will become a kind of small Christian community growing in their faith through prayer, through sharing the Scriptures, and through working together.

Third, as many as possible from the church are involved in small house groups, again using material provided by CMS. Some of these are led by the mission team. This process ends with a parish weekend, at which the missioner preaches at all the masses, encouraging all the parish to be involved in preparing for the mission. He also holds meetings with the mission team to guide them in the practical preparations for the mission, and there is an open meeting on the Sunday afternoon to which all the parish are invited. Throughout this weekend there is a display or exhibition in the church or parish hall. This weekend takes place 5 or 6 months before the mission.

The mission itself is seen as a celebration of faith and of the church. There will be daily masses and evening services, and the missioner or a member of his team will preach at all of these. There will also be evening discussion meetings, a parish social evening, and other special events, for young people, for example.

The aim of the mission is quite wide. It is about drawing in outsiders, but it is also about renewing the faith of the congregation and encouraging them to use their gifts within the church. An opportunity is given for individuals to respond. Frequently a third of the congregation will respond in some way. Most of these, of course, will already be members of the congregation. It must not stop there. Quoting Pope Paul VI: 'The person or the community evangelized then goes on to evangelize others'. CMS usually return to the parish for an open meeting to help the church to develop such a strategy.

The Roman Catholic church has a massive fringe of nominal Christians who nevertheless attend mass. It is a natural strategy for parish missions to focus strongly on the existing congregation, although door-to-door visiting takes place before missions, and members are encouraged to invite their friends. What struck me as so different about the CMS approach was the degree of involvement with the parish before and after the actual mission. Interestingly, a similar approach is taken at the other end of the theological spectrum, in the New Churches. Evangelists are frequently allocated to work with churches over a period of time. We look at this further in chapter 11, when we consider the role of the evangelist.

What is the purpose of a church mission? There may be no one simple answer. Some evangelists, and I believe they are few, have an exceptional gift for 'reaping'. I am not wanting to deflect them from their call. Many of us, though, will have had experience of missions where the brief 'in and out' treatment simply did not work. The congregation did not have confidence in someone they hardly knew. The evangelists did not properly understand the parish or church. Could it be that the way some of us run missions is still geared to the times when churches had massive fringes and there was no effective evangelism going on for the rest of the year?

10 Men's Evangelism

It is well known that there is a shortage of men in churches. Recent published figures for the proportion of male churchgoers in England, Scotland, and Wales were 42%, 37%, and 38%.[1] One reason for believing this imbalance is not *completely* unavoidable is that it does not occur, to anywhere near the same extent, in all churches. According to the 1989 English Church Census, whereas the proportion of men in the Anglican Church was 39%, in the independent churches it was 49%, the same proportion as in the population.

Our concern in this book is the ability of the church to attract and retain adults. With this in mind, the figures need to be adjusted in 2 ways. First, the elderly should not be included. There is a strong age imbalance in favour of women amongst the over 65s, but this is partly caused by women dying later than men. It is not clear to what extent it reflects the church's life and evangelism. I had thought that removing this age group would make my own church, the Church of England, look a little bit better against the independents. Alas, we also need to remove children from the figures for equally obvious reasons. The effect of this is to make the traditional churches look even worse. Table 7 shows the proportions of male churchgoers once those under 15 and over 64 are removed from the figures.

It seems fairly clear that the churches with a more traditional ministry have a higher percentage of women. We shall consider possible reasons for this shortly.

Church of England	36%
URC	37%
Methodists	38%
Afro-Carribbean	40%
Baptists	40%
Roman Catholics	43%
Pentecostals	44%
Independent Churches	50%

Table 7   Percentage of Male Churchgoers Aged 15–64

Several plausible reasons have been put forward for the gender imbalance which has applied, to a greater or lesser extent, in most cultures.[2] These broadly fit into 3 categories. First, there are inherent psychological differences between men and women. It is claimed that men are more independent, possibly more proud, and less aware of need than women. They are also less socially competent, and therefore more easily embarrassed in unfamiliar surroundings. Second are cultural differences. Church can be seen as something for women and children. In working-class areas, in particular, attending church may be seen as effeminate on one hand, or as aping the middle class on the other. Third, there are practical considerations arising from the nature of the church's ministry. For example, women are more available to attend church groups in the day.

First, let us take the inherent and cultural factors together. The important question is whether we can do anything about them. The answer to that *must* be 'yes'. Otherwise, how do the independent churches have equal proportions of men and women? I am not suggesting, incidentally, that they have *no* imbalance, certainly amongst new converts. Independent churches formed too small a sample in my surveys to make any firm claims. Nevertheless, I had no returns from churches claiming more men than women amongst their new Christians. Of the New Churches, the fastest growing sector of the independents, some had an equal balance but others a 40:60 split. I would guess that around 45% of new Christians in the New Churches are men, which is still well ahead of the traditional churches. What is it that they do differently?

One New Church leader suggested to me that the style of leadership was important. Clergy in the traditional churches are selected and trained mainly according to a pastoral model. Many are also more at home in the study than on the sports field. Ministers can be a little bit too safe, too passive, maybe a fraction pompous in the eyes of many men. In the opinion of the leader I was speaking to, the wearing of robes added to this problem. I can certainly believe this, at least amongst those with no church background; but I have no evidence. If the traditional churches were business concerns they would research this as a priority!

If the nature of the leadership may be one reason for the difference, could the style of worship be another? I have no evidence. Frankly, there are elements in both styles of worship which visitors can find off-putting. There is more, however, to the feel of a church than its services. I was speaking to one New Church leader about the range of activities organized by his church. There were meals in pubs, golf days, snooker nights for men, as well as lively events for families. As he talked to me, I realized how this all changed the 'corporate image' of the church. It made it so much easier to talk about at work, for example. I am not, of course, suggesting that it is only the New Churches which organize these kinds of activities, though they are in the forefront. My point is that the events which we shall be considering in this chapter are important not only in their own right, but as they contribute to the overall image of the church in helping to overcome the cultural barriers faced by men.

We now turn to the practical factors. One would expect that Osmosis-style churches would have a higher proportion of women than Web churches. Many of the community groups and other daytime activities of the Osmosis church will draw mainly women. In the first survey, the proportion of women drawn in through community groups was 92%. What is more, the Osmosis church operates on a pastoral model of evangelism, which is likely to draw women.

The research tends to corroborate this expectation. The percentages of men for the four main models, excluding hybrids, are as shown in table 8.

Osmosis	33%
Web	42%
Open Door	40%
Stepping-Stones	37%

Table 8   Percentage of Men Attending Different Types of Church

The sample sizes are a little small (see appendix 2, table A8); nevertheless the general point is made.

Men's Groups

We have seen that most churches are likely to face a shortage of men, and that this will probably be greatest in the Osmosis churches. What can be done? A few years ago I read a couple of books which suggested strongly that it was vital to have a men's group. This should have a dual purpose of fellowship and mission. It should motivate and inspire the Christian men, and should also arrange outreach activities.

I felt guilty that my church at the time did not have such a group, but was confused as to how to proceed. I had no clear vision. We had so few men in our home groups anyway, that it seemed a drastic step to pull out those we did have to form a weekly men's group. I muttered something in our church committee meeting, and someone arranged an occasional gathering in a pub, but we never got very far. I determined to do some research to find out how it worked out in practice for churches which were running successful evangelistic men's groups. The last 2 years has provided such an opportunity.

It needs to be said that most men do not become Christians through a men's group. In the first survey, out of 485 men only 21, or 4%, were significantly influenced by a men's group or events (appendix 2, table A7). Out of 113 churches, only 29 had a men's group, of which 23 included evangelism as an aim (appendix 2, table A3).

I carried out a modest project to investigate men's groups which were successful in evangelism. My most helpful source of contact was Christian Viewpoint for Men, which specializes in helping groups organize men's evangelistic events.[3] I have found other groups 'on the grapevine'. Altogether I have been in touch with 20 groups. The picture is not a particularly encouraging one. Many groups are struggling, and the tension between involvement in the men's group and leadership elsewhere in the church is a real one. Very few groups indeed meet weekly, for the reasons I had experienced.

Nevertheless, some groups are making headway. Let us examine the different types of group, under the headings of Presence, Proclamation and Persuasion. We shall then explore whether there are some principles which need to be followed for a successful strategy for men's evangelism.

Presence Groups

I have come across very few men's groups of a 'Presence' or social nature at all. There are sports teams to be sure. I have not researched them as others are better equipped to do so, and literature is available.[4] I found one valiant men's and toddlers group, meeting on a Saturday morning with roughly equal numbers of men from the church and visitors! There were some men's social groups, usually in quite traditional churches, and serving a valuable function in keeping in touch with the fringe. Usually they were rather static, appealing to mainly older men and with few new members. In one case, though, a good number were drawn into an adult catechumenate group.

I had expected, though, to find many more groups of a social nature, particularly in the working-class areas. These are the areas where there is often a culture gap to be bridged. I had expected to find regular snooker and pool evenings, for example, where men could get to know each other over a pint. I received some glowing accounts of such groups from travelling evangelists and others, but when I investigated them they were always one-off evenings laid on for a mission.

I had also heard of the great value of involving fringe men in practical work on the buildings. I was not sure I would have the cheek to ask them, but I had been assured on a number of occasions that many men would be only too willing to help, and would feel more secure being able to give something in an area where they were competent. I am sure this does happen, but I have only come across one case. This was on a council estate church in North London in the early eighties. The Church Army evangelist Roger Murphy drew in a number of men on Saturday mornings to help with work on the church, and there were many opportunities for the Christians to speak about their faith over cups of coffee. A great deal of practical work needed doing, and the group grew to nearly 30. A social night with pool and other activities was started, meeting about once a month, usually with a speaker. This all went on for about 2 years, leading up to a mission, and about 10 men became Christians over the period.

Why is this kind of thing so rare?

Proclamation Groups

These are the most popular kind of group, and I can see why. Typically, a church will organize 3 or 4 breakfasts or dinners a year, with a speaker. The occasional nature of the meetings makes them viable, both from the point of view of those being invited if they have busy diaries, and for the stretched Christians who run them. They are effective, though we are not talking about revival! Of 12 groups of this type amongst the ones I studied, an average of 2 people a year were becoming Christians.

Virtually all the Christian Viewpoint for Men groups are of this type. Richard Maggs, their national coordinator, estimates that around two-thirds of the groups are based on a regular Saturday morning breakfast. This works well, but appeals in many cases to men in the 45-plus bracket. There are some exceptions, but younger men with families often do not find Saturday morning a good time. Most other groups hold evening dinners.

These events sound, and mostly are, very middle class! Some groups ring the changes to try and draw in a slightly wider clientele. One group holds around 5 main events in a year. There is a smart annual dinner in a hotel; a more informal supper, again with a speaker, in a pub; 2 purely social evenings such as skittles and swimming; and a charity quiz. The socials usually draw about 30 men, the pub evening slightly more, and the annual dinner up to 50. The charity quiz is mixed, with wives and other groups from the church involved, and is much bigger with around 50 teams taking part.

Certainly the formal dinner approach needs to be modified in many parts of the country. On one occasion the men's group at St Mark's, Haydock, near Liverpool, organized a 'hotpot quiz' in a working men's club. It was simply advertised by posters in the club and in 2 shops. In all, 250 turned up, 80% of them not Christians!

Christ the King Church, in Barton Seagrave, near Kettering, organized a tenpin bowling evening. It was followed by chicken and chips in the social area of the Superbowl during which there was a speaker. Fifty people came, including around 30 non-Christians. Seven agreed to take part in a 3-week enquirers' group as a result.

One of the hardest things in organizing this type of event is finding the right speaker. Clergymen are not always a big draw! I have heard of excellent events where a top Christian sportsman has agreed to speak, but these men have such demands on their time it is very few groups who can get them. Christian Viewpoint for Men provide a very helpful list of speakers for affiliated groups, and their joining fee is very reasonable!

Persuasion Groups

One of the keys to success in men's evangelism is building some form of enquirers' group on to the Proclamation event. Let us consider an example of this.

☐ The men's group at Crowborough Parish Church in Sussex consists mainly of middle or senior managers in their 40s and 50s. The centre-piece of the work is a Saturday morning breakfast which is held roughly bimonthly in a reasonably smart hotel. This attracts an average of 50 to 70 men, with perhaps 20 non-Christians. Once a year, an informal enquirers' group is run for about 6 weeks, also on Saturdays and meeting at the same time as the breakfasts. From this group, some join a weekly men's discussion on Monday evenings, and others join the home groups. Occasionally a more structured 'Open to Question' group is also held. By this stage the men are starting to come to church, though some find church services difficult. For some, the men's discussion is really their church.

I find the parallel between the senior executive Crowborough men and the young UPA Hyson Green women (see p. 37) extraordinary. In both cases 'link strategies' are the key, with an enquirers' group involving people they have already got to know of similar age and sex. In both cases some find the move to church difficult. Yet in most ways it would be hard to find more different groups!

Are there any special rules for men's enquirers' groups? Generally, no, though men's evangelist Derek Cook advises that many men want their religion 'up front'. They will want the chance to ask blunt questions. It may, therefore, be wise to highlight this feature of the group in the advertising. A name like 'Open to Question' is a good one.

The biggest difficulty about men's enquirers' groups is an organizational one. Most churches, if they are already organizing an evening enquirers' group, could not afford to split it by holding a separate group for men.

(Stephen Croft, vicar of St George's Ovenden) . . . donned a leather jacket and dark glasses in church one morning and announced the start of a new course

explaining the Christian faith, but this time women were barred. 'To my absolute astonishment 27 men turned up to our first meeting and most of them were non-Christian', he said.[5]

Few men's enquirers' groups could have been more successful than this! Yet the group was not repeated. The group members were enthusiastic, and wanted to keep together, but Stephen felt it would go stale. He could not sustain a men's nurture course and a mixed course as well. The men were fed into the house groups, and are now held together by Saturday breakfasts, a residential weekend each year, and 2 or 3 other events.

One approach is to hold very short men's enquirers' groups, and then to feed those interested into a larger mixed group. Mike Talbot, vicar of Christ the King Church, Kettering, has done this on a number of occasions. A small group of 3 or 4 men are invited to a one-off evening. If they are interested, the group continues for 3 or 4 weeks, looking at issues such as work and family, based on Christian testimony videos. Other events are more informal still, simply attempting to answer questions over a pint of beer. These short-term groups will not answer even half their questions, but it may stimulate enough interest for them to join a more structured group.

The message which comes across is that it is quite helpful to hold the enquirers' group on a men-only basis, but it is not essential. What is absolutely vital is that there is some link from the Proclamation event to a Persuasion group.

Strategic 'Keys'

Are there key principles, as there were for the parent and toddler groups, which we can deduce from the case material for evangelization through men's groups? I believe there are 3 such keys. Interestingly, all of them applied also to the parent and toddler groups.

KEY I AN AGREED EVANGELISTIC AIM

As with parent and toddler groups, I am not suggesting that every men's group should have an evangelistic aim. There is a movement at present of Christian men wanting to meet together in order to develop a greater depth of relationship with each other. I am not suggesting that such groups ought to involve themselves with evangelism. What I am saying is that *if* one of the aims is evangelism it needs to be absolutely clear. One of the difficulties experienced by Christian sport teams, which frequently begin with an evangelistic aim, is that the aim soon drifts simply to playing sport. The Baptist Men's Movement has 2 aims, winning men for Christ and promoting Christian fellowship among men. Over many years the second predominated, and the groups became inward looking. Now most of the groups are quite small, with an average age in the 50s or 60s. These groups meet weekly or perhaps monthly, for fellowship and to listen to a speaker. The national leadership, and many of the local groups, are trying to rediscover their evangelistic edge, but it is extremely difficult once a group has begun to turn inwards.

There is something about a men's group which needs to be transitory. I cannot fully explain it, but it is an impression I have gained talking to the groups. Rather like sailing, leadership needs to constantly adjust the sail settings if they are not to drift away from their purpose.

☐ The men's group at St Mark's, Haydock has been meeting monthly now for about 10 years. Evenings included a talk which has always been intended to appeal to both Christians and uncommitted friends. For example, a recent meeting involved a special branch officer speaking on the drugs problem from a Christian perspective. In recent years, though, the attendance of non-Christians at these meetings has been poor. At quarterly larger events, though, which have been arranged jointly with 2 other churches, the proportion of non-Christians has been much higher, at between 30 and 40%. At the time of writing, the group now plans to abandon the monthly meetings in favour of a fortnightly men's house group, which will include learning to share their faith. Even greater emphasis will be laid on the large quarterly meetings, which will have a specific target of attracting 50% non-Christians. The Haydock group realized that their monthly meetings were falling between 2 stools. They were not effective in evangelism, nor were they of any real value in discipling the Christians. St Mark's realized the need to reset their sails.

KEY 2 EFFECTIVE LINK STRATEGIES

The groups which have had considerable numbers of men becoming Christians are the ones which have been able to channel those sufficiently interested into enquirers' groups. Most of the groups I have studied have had, as their core activity, a number of meals each year with a speaker. Of these, the ones with an enquirers' group have had an average of 15 men become Christians over the last 5 years. The ones without an enquirers' group have had an average of 4 men. I realize there is an element of self-fulfilling prophecy about this, because obviously, if no one is interested, it will not be possible to start an enquirers' group anyway! My analysis therefore falls short of proof. Nevertheless, I believe that the enquirers' groups are a key factor.

How, though, are men to be encouraged to join such groups? There are 2 ways. In most of the groups, the leadership simply gets to know the men well enough to be able to ask them if they will come to a group. This is not as easy as it sounds. You have to steer a line between threatening people and being so polite that you never challenge anyone at all. It needs good leadership.

The other approach is used by the Christian Viewpoint for Men group in Bramhall, near Manchester. This is an interdemoninational group in a middle-class area drawing from several churches. Two men prayed together for more than a year before starting the group. Now they have a lively committee, and 80 to 100 men, half of them non-Christians, gather twice a year for a Saturday breakfast in a hotel. At the end of the talk men are encouraged to complete response slips, which are available on the tables. There is a box to tick if they are interested in joining an 'Open to Question' group meeting on 4 Monday evenings. Usually, half a dozen or so tick this box and join a group, and a fair proportion become Christians as a result.

The point is that no one joins an enquirers' group without being challenged to do so in one way or another.

KEY 3 A COMMITTED TEAM

It became quite clear during my research that the most successful groups were run by a team. They are the ones who can be relied upon to bring non-Christians. The first step in forming an outreach men's group must surely be to gather together a team.

The men's evangelist Jim Smith, however, would wish to go further than this. It is not enough simply to have a core team. The men in the church need to be challenged and enthused. When Jim organizes a men's mission, he encourages the men in the church to gather together for a discipleship course for a year beforehand. He believes the long-term benefits of this to be enormous. While this might not always be possible, the principle must surely be valid. The men in the church must 'own the group'. Unless a high proportion of the Christian men have said they will pray for the outreach meetings and do their best to bring friends, the leadership will have a hard time ahead!

What, though, of the dedicated leader in a hard situation with no one to share his vision? It would be foolish for me to give any glib answers. I can only suggest that in some cases it might be wise to pool resources with like-minded men in other local churches.

11 Motivating the Congregation

I was struck by a splendid picture received by 'Springboard', an Anglican evangelistic initiative, soon after its launch. 'Imagine yourself to be standing holding a bucket of water; on one side of you is a towering inferno, and on the other side 25 sleeping firemen. The question is, which way do you throw the water?'

At the start of the research I asked a church leader with wide experience of the British church what he felt was the question on evangelism that most ministers wanted answering. His answer was that there is one cry he hears over and over again from tired clergy: 'How do we motivate our flock for evangelism?'

Motivation is produced by effective leadership. That is really the subject of another book. There are, however, 3 areas relating to evangelistic strategy and touched on by the research which relate to this vital question of motivation. We consider them in turn.

The Cell Group Approach

The secular management world has been aware for some time that the most effective way of changing the culture in an organization is through small groups. Many churches have an enormous advantage in this respect, in that we have such groups ready formed. Yet the culture of these groups themselves can need changing. Many of them are inward looking, and although they perform a valuable pastoral function they contribute little to evangelism.

Is it possible that these very cells could be injected with a growth enzyme? The largest churches worldwide are all 'cell-group churches', where the small groups draw in new members and multiply of their own accord. The most famous of these, with a membership approaching a million, is the Full Gospel Central Church in Seoul, South Korea. Other enormous churches of this type exist, however, in many parts of the world, particularly in South East Asia and West Africa. Most of them are Pentecostal, but some Roman Catholic churches are also showing an interest in cells. The Parish Church of Milan has grown from 300 to 1,400 members in 3 years using the approach.

For such growth to occur, researchers of the cell group approach are agreed that several aspects of the normal home group culture need to be changed:

1. The cell must be the main sub-unit of the church. A high proportion of the church's membership should be in cells, which should form the very core of church life. Even functions such as finance, music and youth work should be run by specialist cell groups.

2. The cells should be a microcosm of the church. Each member should have a role. They are not passive attenders.

3. Each cell should aim to multiply (this word is considered more positive than 'split' or 'divide'). To this end, it will have an annual goal for the number of non-Christians who will join the group. To help focus the group's attention on this goal, Bill Atwood, an Episcopalian minister from the USA, recommends always having one empty chair in the room as a symbol of those who are still outside the group. On this chair is a list of names for whom they are praying and hoping to invite.

4. Welcoming the new people places quite a demand on the group members. Theological language is banned! Discussion must be practical about how Christian faith affects everyday life. An approach advocated by Ralph Neighbour, another American, is to split the group.[1] One half is a 'share' group; really an enquirers' group for those who are not yet Christians. The other is a 'shepherd' group for those who are Christians, though they are all presumed to be new Christians! The group is meant to multiply every 6 months, after which the shepherd group members will be needed as leaders.

5. It goes without saying that all this places considerable demands on the home group leadership. There is therefore a heavy emphasis on training.

Does this work in Britain? I have to confess I have not found one example where the full cell group dynamic is operating or where the majority of enquirers come in through the cell groups. Some Ichthus Fellowship groups have attempted it. Ichthus Deptford Park, (see p. 49) is certainly an example of a home group which has reached out in a remarkable way. Generally, working-class groups seem more open to outsiders, possibly because their emphasis tends to be on fellowship and pastoral care rather than heavy Bible study, which can frighten newcomers terribly. In general, homogeneous groups will draw others in best. I have found examples of this in ethnic churches, in women's daytime groups and, to an extent, with young people in their 20s.

Even if the full cell-church philosophy is not operating in Britain, many churches are working hard at making their groups more outward-looking. In the early days of the 'house church movement', as it was then called, there was great emphasis on the importance of small fellowship groups, whose main roles were worship, Bible study, fellowship and prayer. Over time, many of them went a little stale. In the early 1980s the Cobham church in the Pioneer network of churches received what they believed was a prophetic message from God that they had become rather like a luxury cruise liner when God wanted them to be a battleship. Everything was too cosy. They were enjoying each other's fellowship, but they were not getting on with the task of evangelism which God had given them. The groups were restructured, and all now have a task. Where possible, 2 or 3 groups in an area gather together to form an evangelism team. These teams have different roles, but they always involve some kind of outreach. It could be youth work, or door-to-door visiting, or starting a new Sunday morning congregation in an area. It might contain a strong element of social action, for example working with the elderly. All the groups still meet for fellowship and Bible study as they used to, but even those which cannot combine to form an evangelism team now have an evangelistic aim. For example, they will arrange home group social events to which outsiders are invited.

Anyone who has tried to change the culture of a church's home groups will know that it is not easy. One Anglican vicar, Tony Higton, and his wife Patricia, based on their experience in Hawkwell parish, have produced a course to help churches make the transition. This course known as TIME (Together for Intercession, Ministry, and Evangelism)[2] lasts for 20 weeks and is done by all the home groups in a church. The aim is to make sure that, as far as possible, all church members are agreed on the church's vision which will include every member ministry and the importance of outreach. At the end of the course there is a dedication service for those who feel able to commit themselves to the church's vision.

This, however, is only the beginning. There is a change in emphasis for the home groups, which become 'ministry groups'. By the end of 2 years, while 2 weeks in the month will be for receiving through fellowship and teaching, the other 2 weeks will be for giving out. Typically, one of these weeks will be spent planning or actually running some type of evangelism; the other week will be for prayer and administration of practical and pastoral jobs.

I have been in touch with 3 churches which have used the TIME approach during my research, and they have all been enthusiastic. There have been definite benefits in terms of involving more people in ministry, and there has been a marked increase in prayer. People still find evangelism difficult, but the home groups have certainly become more outward-looking. Evangelism has not necessarily been to draw people into the home group itself. At Christ Church, Bridlington, for example, one group runs a monthly evangelistic dinner in a hotel. The whole church can bring people to this, but the home group does the organization, and people become Christians as a result.

The particular course used by TIME has a charismatic evangelical emphasis. I am not suggesting it would be appropriate for every church. Nevertheless, for any church with a developed system of home groups, the use of a course to help the church become more outward looking seems a natural approach.

The Training Approach

There is nothing which encourages a fisherman like catching a fish! There is no doubt that much of people's reticence about evangelism comes from lack of confidence. Few things will give them that confidence, and indeed help them to trust God, more than being involved in front-line evangelism. This can take many forms: sending faith sharing teams to another church; encouraging the young people to help on summer camps and house parties; or involving people in a form of evangelism in the church.

The great advantage of Evangelism Explosion, and also of Good News Down the Street, is that in different ways they train people to be evangelists by doing. This was the method Jesus used with his disciples. It has been called the 'apprenticeship method'.

☐ Abertridwr Community Church is situated in a rural area near Caerphilly in South Wales. In 1983 the church had 21 adults. By 1993 this had grown to 120. 80% of the growth was from new Christians through Evangelism Explosion. The church has now held 11 EE training programmes. Altogether 65 members have been trained. Most of them were very timid when they started the course, and felt they would scarcely be able to handle the book-learning aspect, let alone going into someone's home to share their faith. The church now has difficulty in finding enough fringe contacts for course members to visit, but there is no doubt that Evangelism Explosion has revolutionized the Christians. They are more certain of their faith, and have much more confidence in sharing it.

The confidence came through the apprentice method. Both EE and Good News Down the Street use a 1-2-3 approach. Number 1 is the team leader and is fairly experienced. Number 2 has perhaps been a member of a team once or twice before, and would normally contribute a certain amount in the sessions. Number 3 has probably never been part of a team before, is terrified, but need not say a word!

We have seen that persistence is needed to get EE running effectively in a church (p. 80). Nevertheless, the motivational effect of this approach can be enormous. The EE material is strongly evangelical in flavour, but there is no reason why other materials should not be produced using the apprentice method. The Roman Catholic evangelization course referred to on p. 81, which can be used as a way in to the adult catechumenate, is an example of this.

Through Staffing

One way to tell the priorities of any organization is to see whom it employs. If a church takes evangelism seriously it will employ evangelists, and in chapter 9 we have seen examples of the impact they have in some of the New Churches. Indeed, it has been a claim of the New Churches from the beginning that they take seriously the 5-fold ministries (apostles, prophets, evangelists, pastors, and teachers) of Ephesians 4. They see it as a considerable point of weakness in most traditional churches that we limit our staffing almost entirely to pastor-teachers.

Let me give some statistics from 2 of the New Churches. In the New Frontiers network, there are 100 churches. Their staffing includes 40 evangelists, approximately 30 of whom are employed full-time. All the New Frontiers churches are covered by an evangelist in one way or another.

In the Pioneer network, at least 50% of all full-time workers are in evangelism. Of those currently going into full-time ministry, there are about 2 evangelists for every pastor-teacher. They are employed in a wide range of work. Some work in schools and with young people; others are involved leading and training the teams of volunteers, mainly young people, who give maybe a year to work for the church; others are employed in the churches, helping and motivating the Christians to share their faith.

It is a case of the apprentice method writ large. Just as great footballers make others want to play football, and great preachers might even make others want to preach, so gifted evangelists with a passion for helping people to become Christians encourage others to do the same.

We have seen that in the Pioneer network of churches 50% of non-administrative staff are employed as evangelists. In the Church of England I estimate the comparable percentage to be 2%, and there must be a similar percentage in most of the traditional churches. Even allowing for those in mainly pastoral roles who also carry out some effective evangelism, the difference is extraordinary. Is it not an indicator of the importance we attach to evangelism?

PART 3
Towards a Strategy

In part 2 we considered the tactics or 'nuts and bolts' of evangelism. We saw how these can vary in different kinds of church depending, in particular, on whether the church has a Personal or Institutional fringe. The reader may find it helpful to refer again to the diagram on p. 25 to regain a sense of overall perspective, and also as a reminder of the likely different 'ways in' for the different models of church. In the light of this information we shall summarize the main models of evangelization in chapter 13 prior to looking at strategy formulation in the final chapter.

First, in chapter 12, we need to consider a question which may seem a fraction technical. Some readers may wish to skip it. Nevertheless it is important if we are to have a realistic view of the growth potential for any particular church from pursuing Web strategies.

12 Growth Dynamics and Web Churches

Why is it that every church does not work from a Personal fringe, particularly given the dramatic growth experienced by some of the Web churches? It is easy to see how the size of the Institutional fringe may vary from church to church, but do we not all have friends? Do not the Osmosis and Open Door models, which depend primarily on an Institutional fringe, imply that for some reason their members have no relationships with those outside the church? We can put it more strongly. Does not the very notion of an Institutional fringe smell of clericalism? Are not the Osmosis and Open Door churches ones in which the members are failing in their duty to spread the gospel, and draw in their friends?

There may, of course, be some truth in these accusations. There may be a number of reasons why a church is not growing through its Personal fringe. The nature of the services may simply not be appealing to enquirers; the underlying spirituality may not emphasize evangelism; or the church members may have become so engrossed in church activities that they have lost all interest in those outside. Nevertheless, we need to understand that growth through a Personal fringe is very much easier in some churches than others.

In commuter areas, for example, many of the men and the working women may know few people locally whom they could invite to church. The 'feel' of the church can also be a factor. It may be easier to invite a work colleague, who may need to travel 3 or 4 miles, to a city centre church than to a small housing estate church which is clearly intended for that local community.

Similarly, churches where most of the members have been Christians for many years can face a problem. It is true, the fault may lie partly with them for being inward looking. Nevertheless, there can come a time when most of our contacts have been invited to church events, and have said 'no'! At a certain age it is not as easy to make new friends as when we were students. I know of people who have deliberately cut down on church activities and joined evening classes, for example, in an effort to build up relationships with non-Christians. This is worthwhile and praiseworthy, but we must concede that personal circumstances will make it hard for some. I have not yet heard of a British church where this kind of approach has had a dramatic effect on evangelization.

There is a cut-off level of relationships which the church needs if it is to achieve sustained growth from the Personal fringe. Appendix 3 contains a simplified model of how a church may grow through friendship links, depending on the number of friends its members have, their receptivity to the gospel, and the proportion who live within range of the church. The model allows for a distinction between new Christians and established Christians. It is well known that new Christians are likely to have many more unchurched friends, and some of them in practice will be more open to the gospel for 2 reasons. First, the friends of the established Christians who are really open should have been converted years ago! More important, there is something fresh about a new Christian. Others can see the change in their life. Their friends may not be inherently any more open, but some of them will become so because of the change in their friend.

The worked example in appendix 4 shows the comparative growth of 3 very similar churches. Figure 6 illustrates this. The only differences are that for churches B and C twice as many friends live in the catchment area as for church A, and for church C the population is twice as receptive to the gospel as for churches A and B. The differences in church growth are staggering. All churches start with 100 members. Church A grows slowly over 15 years and hits a plateau at 116. In the last year it has 6 converts. Church B's rate of growth increases yearly, and after 15 years it has grown to 631 members, with 105 converts in the last year. Church C experiences even more dramatic growth, reaching a congregation of 12,000 in 11 years! (Such growth is, of course, unknown in Britain, though not overseas.)

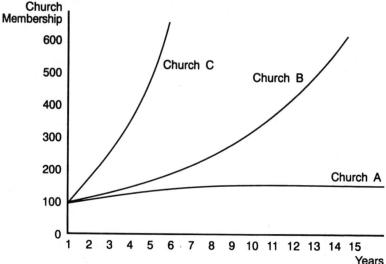

Figure 6   Patterns of Church Growth

The reader may question the validity of such a simplified model. A degree of caution in interpreting the results from it is, of course, necessary. Nevertheless, one needs to be clear about the purpose of this type of modelling. It is not to predict any result *per se*, but to test the sensitivity of the result to changes in particular variables. Readers can construct their own models – or experiment with this one. A few minutes with a calculator should demonstrate the dramatic sensitivity of the rate of growth in a Web church to the receptivity (and sociability) of the population, to the number of friends of its members, and to the proportion of such contacts who live within the catchment area of the church.

The model demonstrates that it is much easier for some churches than others to build their overall growth on their Personal fringe. That is not to say the others can sit back. Every church has some Personal fringe and, even under the Osmosis model, friendships will be one of the most important constituents in evangelization, even if their role is sometimes as a supportive factor. Nevertheless, growth from the Personal fringe will only normally 'take off' when a church has a substantial catchment area with a receptive population.

A second area where the model provides some insights is in understanding why church growth tends to level out at a ceiling.

Ceilings

St Hilda's is an ordinary church in an ordinary town. It is slightly more effective than average. The cause of this need not concern us. It may be due to the prayers of its people or the gifts of its minister or the fortunate site of its building. The fact is, it is steadily growing. Is there any reason why it should not keep on growing? It currently has 200 members, and this number has grown by 20 in the last year. Is there any reason why, in the next 50 years, it should not have grown by a further 1,000? We all know it will not do so. What, though, is the dynamic which will stop St Hilda's growth?

Most writing on such ceilings has concentrated on constraints operating within the internal life of the church. Using a parallel with economics, they have concentrated on supply. The usual causes are:

1. The size of the building. There is a much quoted principle that churches stop growing when they are 80% full. Supposedly, the congregation then lose their incentive to bring new people. I have heard it rumoured that this rule is based on no more than an 'off the cuff' comment by an authority on church growth, and that the so-called research evidence has grown with the telling! Be that as it may, the '100% rule' is certainly valid. People will be deterred from coming if they cannot get a seat.

2. The management capacity of the minister and the other full-time staff.

3. Difficulties of communication and strain in relationships once a church grows beyond about 200 people, unless supporting pastoral structures are in place.[1]

In this author's opinion, the cause of ceilings is 2-fold. Keeping to economics terminology, they can be due to supply or to demand. All the suggested internal (supply) reasons can indeed apply. For some reason, though, the demand side, the dynamics of evangelism, have usually been neglected.[2] We have just seen the phenomenon simply demonstrated using the mathematical model, where Church A quickly reached a plateau when the small number of people joining the church through evangelism was equalled by the excess of leavers over joiners.

Let us consider how the size and existence of ceilings might vary for the 5 models of church we have considered so far. For the Osmosis and Open Door churches the maximum size will inevitably be determined by staffing. These churches are strongly dependent on clergy input. In practice, it is almost unheard of for them to grow beyond about 500 people. Using terminology introduced by David Wasdell,[3] 'lay mission' is limited by demand, and 'clergy mission' is limited by supply. A slightly different analysis applies for the Stepping-Stones church, but with the same result. There is a limit to the size and number of social and other events which a church can organize. Also, since the Stepping-Stone church normally operates in an unreceptive population, it may face limitations from demand as well. In practice all these 3 models of church are unlikely to grow beyond about 500. In the case of the Web and the Budding models, however, there is no limitation on the supply side, and in a receptive population the scope for growth is enormous. The biggest constraint faced by these churches in practice is size of buildings, although Web churches can also feel strains in church organization.

It will not have escaped the reader's notice that all this has immense implications for evangelistic strategy.

Implications for Church Planting

Church planting is a vital and substantial topic in its own right. It is quite outside the scope of this book to explore it in any detail. I wish, simply, to show how the study of evangelism dynamics and growth ceilings can shed light on a phenomenon which is not generally understood.

The story of many church plants goes something like this. Fifty people leave the parent church to start a daughter church meeting in a school on a housing estate. There is much enthusiasm, and there is some initial growth as some receptive contacts are drawn in. After a while, though, things settle down and the church hits a ceiling. Nevertheless, the places left vacant in the parent church are quickly filled, and another 'plant' may even be attempted. There is little agreement, though, as to why the first plant has stagnated.

There may, of course, be more than one reason. The daughter may, for example, lack some of the 'open doors' to the community of its parent. The thinking in the last section, however, suggests that one important limitation is likely to be a 'demand side' restriction arising from a low proportion of the congregation's contacts being in the church's catchment area. The growth in the parent church is through relaxation of 'supply side' restrictions, usually space and ministerial time.

A considerable volume of most valuable literature has come out recently on church planting. I should like to make one observation. Nothing I have read lays much stress on the relationship in terms of evangelism dynamics between the parent and daughter churches. Yet it is vital to the strategy. Let us suppose the parent church is a thrusting, fast growing Web. Will the daughter church also be such a fast growing plant, or will it be a gentle Osmosis church, soon reaching a ceiling in a small self-contained community? What are the expectations of the core group? The difference in the likely results could not be greater. Both approaches may be valid, but clear thinking early on should help planning and could also avoid disappontment due to unrealistic expectations.

13 Models of Evangelization

We have spoken already of the existence of different models of evangelization. Four main ones have been considered – Osmosis, Open Door, Web and Stepping-Stone – and a fifth type, the Budding model, has been mentioned briefly. Case examples have been given but, to an extent, the reader has been asked to take their existence on trust. No research evidence has so far been presented.

In this chapter we first consider some evidence for the existence of the 4 main models. We then summarize the characteristics of these and also some additional models which the reader may have discovered in the case material earlier in the book.

Research Evidence

The reader will recall that the existence of the 4 models was proposed as a result of evidence distilled from the first survey. In the second survey, ministers were asked to categorize their churches according to the models. How well did the categories fit?

It will be seen from table A8 in appendix 2 that they fitted reasonably well. Out of 66 churches, 48 were classed as being pure versions of one model; 17 were hybrids; only one minister felt unable to classify his church according to any of the models.

Table 9 summarizes the characteristics of the pure, as opposed to the hybrid, models from the two surveys.

It will be seen from table 9 that the majority of churches depended upon an Institutional rather than a Personal fringe. Forty-seven were Osmosis or Open Door churches as against 19 which were Web or Stepping-Stone churches.

There is little difference in average size of congregation for the models in table 9. This is not surprising since the sizes involved are well below those at which a ceiling dynamic would be expected to operate. Nevertheless, if the 75% quartile[1] is considered rather than the median, a sharper difference emerges with the Web churches being considerably larger than the other types.

As table 10 suggests, it may be that, even for the modest sizes of congregation we are considering, some degree of the ceiling effect described in the last chapter is starting to operate.

	No. of Churches	Size (No. of Adults)[1]	Growth %[2]	Converts %[3]	Median Community[4]	Visibility[5]	% Converts Local[6]	Nature of Fringe[7]
Osmosis	29	120	$2\frac{1}{2}$%	17%	4	3	51–75%	Even
Open Door	18	127	2%	23%	$3\frac{1}{2}$	3	76–100%	Inst.
Web	11	140	20%	30%	3	2	0–25%	Personal
Stepping-Stones	8	144	22%	31%	3	3	76–100%	Personal

Table 9 Characteristics of Churches

Notes 1 Average adult Sunday attendance
2 Growth in average adult attendance over 5 years
3 Number of new committed Christians in last 5 years as percentage of adult attendance
4 Sense of community rated 1 to 5 (5 high)
5 Visibility of church to local community rated 1 to 5 (5 high)
6 The percentage of new Christians from the parish or within 1 mile of the church
7 Mainly Institutional, even mixture or mainly Personal.

	Size (No. of adults) 75% quartile
Osmosis	130
Open Door	175
Web	270
Stepping-Stones	155

Table 10   Church Size and Style of Evangelism

The Web and Stepping-Stone churches, which operate through a Personal fringe, have a higher average growth rate and are also more effective in producing new Christians than the Osmosis and Open Door churches. That is not to suggest all the Osmosis and Open Door churches were ineffective. There were fast-growing churches with good numbers of new Christians in all categories. In the case of the Osmosis churches, though, success was correlated with the strength of community in the parish or area. The top four Osmosis churches averaged growth over the 5-year period of 20%, and gained new Christians equal to 37% of adult attendance during the same period. Three out of the 4 ministers of these churches rated the sense of community in the area as 5, the highest possible.

The characteristics of the churches – in terms of sense of community, visibility to the community, the proportion of the converts from the local area, and the nature of the fringe – were broadly as one might expect. It is interesting, though not surprising, that the Osmosis churches were described as having an even mixture of Personal and Institutional fringe. In close communities these 2 types of fringe overlap greatly. The Open Door churches, which rely least of all on a Personal fringe, had a very high percentage of new Christians from the local area, as one would expect. The Web churches, also as expected, drew their new Christians from outside the community through the Personal fringe. The Stepping-Stone churches drew a slightly higher percentage of their converts from the local area than one might have expected, but this is based on a smallish sample of only 8 churches.

Bearing in mind that no church represents a completely pure form of any of the models, and that the categorization of the churches into the different models had to rely on subjective judgement, the findings from the surveys supported the existence of the 4 models.

Summary of the Models

Let us now summarize the models we have encountered. The purpose is a diagnostic one. The aim is to provide readers with a check-list to assist understanding of their own church's evangelistic dynamic – both as it is, and as it could be. We shall see that the role of the full-time staff varies considerably.

THE OSMOSIS CHURCH

We have already seen that the Osmosis church is the commonest type. Its underlying philosophy assumes a reasonably cohesive community, and in practice it depends on this for its evangelization. As the research progressed I gained the impression that the Osmosis churches could be subdivided further into 2 categories: Osmosis-passive and Osmosis-active.

An Osmosis-passive church typifies the pure Osmosis philosophy (see p. 20). It is represented well by a note from one Anglican vicar:

> *I have been a parochial clergyman for 37 years and have found on the whole that deliberate attempts to evangelize people just do not work, which may be no excuse for not trying them. Most people coming newly to church seem to have been moved to do so by something in their experience not known to me. Likewise with the people who give up. Thus I have come to rely on a 'laissez-faire' policy though obviously encouraging those who come.*

I suspect he spoke for many. Interestingly, he rated the sense of community in his parish as 5, the highest possible.

This viewpoint has been predominant in my own church, the Church of England, for many years. I hope I have made it clear that I have deep respect for the spirituality and pastoral care which usually accompany it. As we have seen, though, it presumes a certain degree of background Christian faith and identification with the church amongst the population. Without it, even when critical life experiences occur, there is little likelihood of people turning to their local church.

The Osmosis-active church is similar in many respects, but finds the need to be more action-oriented in its approach. This need may result from having a less well-developed fringe, or possibly through being in a more fragmented community. The church seeks to draw people in through a variety of routes, none of which proves to be dominant. It resembles the Open Door church, though with many small doors slightly ajar rather than one or two main ways in.

In both types of Osmosis church the key staff emphasis with regard to evangelization is attempting to be a spiritual focus and pastoral presence in the community.

THE OPEN DOOR CHURCH

The Open Door church is really a modification of the Osmosis model. It operates primarily through the Institutional fringe, but it has found one or two significant 'Open Doors' to make effective contact with the community. As a result, unlike the Osmosis church, it may be able to evangelize effectively even when there is little sense of community in the area.

The most frequently occurring open doors, particularly for Anglican churches, were the 'occasional offices' of weddings, baptisms, and funerals. The most effective of these, as we saw in chapter 7, was baptism preparation. Other open doors included weekly family services, church schools, a children's holiday club, a drop-in centre and a church-run nursery school. Some churches mentioned enquirers' groups or the adult catechumenate, but this involved a misunderstanding. The 'Open Door' refers to the means of significant first contact, not the method of subsequent evangelization.

The key staff emphasis for evangelism will be similar to that of the Osmosis church, but, in addition, identifying and exploiting the Open Door will clearly be a crucial role.

THE WEB CHURCH

As we have seen, the Web church has a straightforward dynamic, with evangelism operating down relationship networks. The point of first contact is usually a Sunday service, which simplifies organization immensely, and thereby removes one major ceiling to growth. I would also classify a church such as Holy Trinity, Brompton, where the main point of first contact is currently the Alpha course, as a Web, as there is still one central focal point enabling the organization to be kept simple.

We have seen that nearly all the large churches in the UK are Webs, the largest being Kensington Temple, an Elim Pentecostal church in London with a total congregation of 5,000.

The fact that enquirers' first contact with the Web church will be a 'religious' occasion such as a service has 2 implications. First, the standard of presentation will need to be high. Second, it will only draw those who are moderately receptive, though it may draw them from a considerable area.

There will be 2 key staff emphases. The first of these will be maintaining a very high standard of preaching and general presentation in services. Second, much time and effort will need to be given to training and equipping the Christians, since it is the ordinary church members who are the prime evangelists in a Web church. Staff will have little time for visiting in the local community, though, if growth takes off, the very presence of large numbers of enquirers and new Christians will produce its own quite heavy counselling load.

THE STEPPING-STONE CHURCH

As we have seen, the Stepping-Stone model is an adaptation of the Web. It usually operates more locally than the Web, in an 'ordinary' church which may be quite mixed as regards age and background. Social and other events are used as stepping-stones to enable people to move towards faith and the church in manageable steps. This enables the Stepping-Stone church to evangelize effectively in a less receptive population than the Web. The more complex mode of operation will place a ceiling on its growth, possibly in the region of 300 people. It does not usually operate on the homogeneous unit principle amongst a receptive group. If it did so, it would quickly become a Web.

Since it operates locally, a Stepping-Stone church will frequently be something of a hybrid with either the Osmosis or Open Door. Roughly 50% fell into this category in the research. This means that it is hard to identify a key staff emphasis. Ministers of Stepping-Stone churches will need to be generalists. They will pastor their own congregation. They will, ideally, have a presence in the community too. In addition, they will need to inspire and envision the Christians to witness to their friends and to bring them to the various events organized by their church.

THE BUDDING MODEL

This model is the most effective of all for incorporating new Christians. It requires an even more receptive population than the Web, and this author is not aware of it operating effectively in Britain. Nevertheless, if major spiritual revival breaks out it is the only model which will be capable of containing the growth.

For the model to operate, the church needs to be radically reorganized to make the cell groups central to all of its life. The culture of these groups needs to be such that enquirers can be invited to join them directly. As groups grow, they divide and multiply. Thus there is no ceiling to growth.

The key staff emphasis for effective evangelization is in training the cell group leaders. The cell group culture needs to be so different from that normally found that the church leadership will need to believe passionately in the approach if it is to succeed.

We have now briefly summarized the 5 models of church already referred to near the start of the book in chapter 3. We now include 3 further models unearthed by the research.

THE SHEPHERD TEAM

A shepherd team involves a central committed group in the church who are the key factor in a church's evangelization of the surrounding area. There are plenty of examples in history. One could point to Jesus and the 12, though arguably their role was pre-evangelism; the reader may be familiar with the role of the monastic orders in the original evangelization of Britain; more recently, also in this country, Anglican churches with large numbers of curates operated on the same principle. The main emphasis in their work was visiting the flock, but the 'flock' included a very large fringe. Much of what was involved was really evangelization.

The reduction, proportionately, in the number of clergy has meant that this model is rare in Britain today. Nevertheless, it does exist, and may even be experiencing something of a comeback. The case study on Ichthus Christian Fellowship, Deptford Park (see p. 49) provides one example. New churches and others which make use of teams of young people who give their time, usually unpaid, provide others. The case study on the Lantern Church, Canford Magna, on p. 45 shows that it can even happen in the Church of England!

I do not believe that the shepherd team is adequate as a model on its own. It must go hand in hand with an underlying dynamic such as the Stepping-Stone or Open Door. Its very existence, though, is a challenge to think big. Jesus told Christians to pray for workers to go into the harvest fields. In some communities the ordinary church members may be able to fulfil this role, but in others full-time help will be needed. The shepherd team churches have had faith to pray for such help.

In summary, the distinctive characteristic of the shepherd team is that the key staff emphasis is direct contact with non-Christians – much more so than for the Osmosis church, and in direct contrast to the Web.

THE FISHING SCHOOL

A fishing school is a church where evangelism training becomes so central to a church's life that it provides a powerful evangelism dynamic of its own. The churches I have come across which most fit this category are some of those using Evangelism Explosion.

This may seem an inconsistent use of words. The other models were defined by the means of first contact rather than by the method of subsequent evangelization. EE, as a form of Persuasion evangelism, relates to the last steps of someone coming to faith rather than the first. Nevertheless, EE provides two things: an extremely flexible way of making use of those contacts which do arise; and a great incentive to the minister and others to find some contacts. The combination of these can be sufficiently powerful to produce, in effect, a separate model.

The importance of the model, as with the shepherd team, is that it can operate with an Institutional fringe even where there is little sense of community in the area. A community with a developed network of relationships will help any form of evangelism, but approaches based on personal evangelism, such as EE, will suffer less if it is not present than those which focus on the church.

THE SLEEPING GIANT

The name – the Sleeping Giant – came to me when reading *Awakening the Giant*, a book on evangelism by a Roman Catholic author with Catholics in mind.[2] My immediate and prejudiced reaction was to agree heartily with the author, 'Yes, the Roman Catholic Church *is* a Sleeping Giant!' It did not take me long to realize that the same can be said of most churches in Britain, my own included, when we compare them with what they could be. I include it as the last category on our check-list because I believe the very name is an encouragement. Giants can awake! Perhaps the reader's church does not fit any of the other models for the simple reason that very little effective evangelism is taking place. The temptation would be to classify it as a sleeping mouse. It is not. It is a giant!

Implications for Leadership

The biggest decision most churches make is appointing a minister. Much too often the result is disastrous. A gifted man or woman goes to a good church but somehow it does not work. There can be more than one reason, of course, but one cause is a failure to understand the very different role which ministers play in different churches, particularly with regard to evangelism. A new minister comes to St Alpho's, a city centre church which has relied, previously, on guest services and the preaching gift of the previous minister. The new man or woman, by contrast, is a personal evangelist. Is the church ready for the change? Have they realized that the very process by which new Christians are drawn in is likely to change as a result? This may mean that a new type of people or age group will predominate, changing the very character of the church. The stresses and strains this process brings to the internal dynamics of church life are rarely understood.

Similarly, the previous minister at St Alpho's, whom everyone was so happy with, may hit problems when he moves to St Beto's, an Osmosis church. The new congregation will doubtless appreciate his preaching gift, but it will be less important than at St Alpho's. Their prime expectation may be that he should be a loving pastor, and someone who spends much time visiting and making contacts in the local community. This is simply not his concept of what ministry is all about. Once again, frustration can set in.

The point is a simple one. One of the times when it is most critical for a church to understand its own evangelism dynamic is when appointing full-time staff, particularly a new minister.

14 Choosing a Strategy

Planning is not as easy in practice as in the management textbooks. When you read about it it can sound deceptively easy. First you set long-term goals. Next you analyse the shifts and trends and needs in the environment, in our case the local community. Next, you appraise the strengths and weaknesses of the organization, in our case the local church. You then devise long- and short-term plans to put right weaknesses where necessary, and to build on strengths in order to meet the long-term goals.

About 20 years ago, I read an article about a new approach to strategic planning. It had a short, snappy name: 'Disjunctive Incrementalism'! It was written by 2, I am sure, incredibly learned American business professors, and I could only understand about one in 3 of the words they used. Nevertheless, by the end of the article I understood what they were saying. The future was so uncertain that, in practice, it was not possible to set long-term goals. The best that could be done was to respond as flexibly as possible to opportunities and problems as they occurred. That was the meaning of 'Disjunctive Incrementalism', though later they gave it an alternative title – 'muddling through'. They claimed it was an approach particularly appropriate to local authorities!

I know the feeling. In practice, in our churches, there is bound to be a great deal of muddling through. We will make mistakes. Crisp strategies will not always pop up when we want them to solve our problems.

Robert Warren, until recently vicar of St Thomas Crookes, in Sheffield, gives an account of how that church wrestled with finding God's strategy in his book *On the Anvil*.[1] The title points to the fact that it was not a pain-free process! The church grew remarkably, and now has over 1,000 worshippers on a Sunday, and also spawned the famous Nine O'Clock Service, a youth congregation which has now become a church in its own right. Robert found that there were 3 ingredients necessary for learning from God and for finding the way forward for a church: intuition, inspiration, and analysis. Intuition referred to our natural human instinct and common sense. Inspiration included direct prophetic messages from God as well as guidance from Scripture. St Thomas's is a strongly charismatic church, yet it is interesting that significant guidance only came through prophecy about 3 times, though on each occasion it was very important. The third category, analysis, is what this book has been about – using our God-given minds, to the best of our ability, to God's glory. Robert Warren expresses the 3 elements as vertices of a triangle.[2]

In this chapter I shall continue to talk about the analysis, but I do not want to give an impression either of over-simplifying the process or of forgetting God! I fully recognize that life will never be as simple as it sounds in this or any book. There will need to be hours of discussing and praying, of listening to God and our fellows. All 3 vertices of Robert Warren's triangle will need to be present.

Where Are We Now?

All are agreed that the first step in planning, as in map reading, must be to find out where you are now. This is the heart of the technique known as 'mission audit'. I shall say little on this subject as other good literature is available.[3]

A mission audit usually involves a great deal of discussion by members of the congregation. Its aim is to discover the strengths and weaknesses of the church. There is usually help from an outside adviser. It is an excellent approach for finding all sorts of practical changes which need to be made for the church to be more welcoming and responsive to the community. As a 'bottom up' approach it also has the advantage of generating commitment to change from the congregation. The ideas have come from them, they are not imposed. For most congregations, though, some external input will be needed in proposing creative strategies for evangelization. The aim of this book is to provide such input.

To supplement this process I should like to suggest 3 additional questions which are not usually included in mission audit material. They are all concerned with understanding the underlying evangelism dynamic. First, where is the church on the 'S' curve which we considered on p. 8. If it is very low indeed on the curve, the real problem is not evangelism at all. The church needs new life. Playing around with strategy will not resolve a problem of fundamental spirituality. Equally, if the church is at the very top of the curve, and is facing constraints due to lack of staff or buildings, evangelism is hardly the problem. In this case, though, the leadership are probably only too well aware of the fact. Between these points, broadly speaking, the higher the church is on the curve, the greater the emphasis that needs to be placed on Persuasion evangelism. If the church is low on the curve, it is further back in the evangelistic process and needs to place more emphasis on Presence and Proclamation.

Second, assuming people have been regularly coming to faith, what has been the dominant model using the check-list presented in the last chapter? It is critical to understand this. I have met church leaders facing disappointment and frustration simply through not understanding that their church was a Web rather than an Osmosis church. I can think of ministers of nonconformist churches who are trying hard to become churches for the local community when nearly all their congregation have come from far afield through a Web process. Of course, it is possible that this is what God is calling them to do; but ministers in such a position need to understand the immensity of the task. They are virtually starting afresh, and by doing so are effectively deciding not to use the evangelistic pulling power of their Personal fringe – the only fringe they currently have.

To understand reliably which is the underlying dynamic, it goes without saying that it is necessary to have reasonably accurate records of how people have become Christians. Yet almost no ministers keep such information. Surely, it must be desirable to have some kind of list of those who have recently come to faith in order to pray for them. I urge readers to consider keeping what records they can.

Third, it is necessary to estimate the strengths and weaknesses of the church's evangelism in '3 P' terms. This is not difficult. Is there a large fringe, or does the church never see a non-Christian? In the latter case, there is clearly a need for Presence and Profile evangelism. Are people apparently becoming Christians and then 'dropping out'? This would suggest there is some successful Proclamation evangelism which is not being followed up properly with a nurture or enquirers' group. Clearly the emphasis needs to be on Persuasion evangelism.

Looking Forward

REMOVING THE BLOCKS

The main emphasis in this book has been on identifying opportunities for evangelism which will be most effective for a particular church and community. At the risk of repetition, I must emphasize that this cannot happen in isolation. The church is an organism. Evangelism will mean change to that organism. It will require committees and secretarial help and a management structure for the church. If, for example, there are so many committees that everything gets bogged down in bureaucracy, or if there are no committees so there is no mechanism for making and implementing decisions, the result will be frustration. Similarly, if the services are boring, or the public address system does not work, or the church is unwelcoming, or there are no home groups for the new Christians, evangelistic initiatives will achieve little. I will say no more. These are all areas where a mission audit can be invaluable. In what follows we assume the church, while doubtless far from perfect, is taking steps to remove any major blocks to growth.

EVANGELISM

The next step is to consider the options for evangelism. It may be worth referring back to part 2 of this book and making a list of the main approaches which could be relevant to the reader's church. Almost certainly, the list will be dauntingly long! It will, of course, only be possible to implement a fraction of the ideas contained in the case material in a book such as this one. There is a limit to the number of new initiatives which any church can carry out, and it will be necessary to set priorities. With this in mind, I suggest 3 key questions which need to be asked at this stage.

First, is there an 'Open Door'? This is the most likely way forward for most Osmosis churches, but it may mean concentrating on one area of ministry for a time, to the comparative exclusion of others. As I write this chapter, I have just started as vicar of a new church, St Mary's, Greenham, near Newbury. Like any new minister I feel excited and sometimes a little overwhelmed by the many different opportunities for ministry. In my judgement, infant baptism couples are the 'Open Door' with the greatest potential at the present time, but much work will be needed by me and others to open the door. I am conscious that I may need to hold back a little from some of the other areas until the priority door is opened – or until I discover that I have made a mistake!

Second, is there a receptive group which can be tapped into by means of Web strategies? This may be a difficult decision area. The existence of such a group does not necessarily mean that it should be the role of my church, or yours, to launch headlong into evangelizing them. At Greenham there has been a long history of youth ministry, based on a youth club in the church hall. We have links with many unchurched teenagers, and there are many others in their 20s in the area who remember the club with affection. Should we start an Alpha Course targeted towards teens or early 20s? We have some gifted youth leaders, but they are a very small group. Would it overstretch us to take on this extra challenge? Would the young people come anyway? Would our church be able to support the new Christians and involve them fully in the church family? The answers to such questions may be no more straightforward in the reader's church than in mine, but they must at least be asked. We have seen that, in the right circumstances, Web strategies yield the greatest evangelistic results of all.

At the risk of digressing, I need to make an important point here. We have seen that, as churches reach a certain size, often around 300, most of the models start to hit a ceiling. The main exception is the Web. It follows that, as churches get to that kind of size, they need to place increasing emphasis on Web strategies. This is not to suggest that they need to become Webs in an overall sense. For many that would be impossible or undesirable. They need, however, to place increasing emphasis on the Personal fringe – or else to plant a new church. Otherwise they will meet frustration.

To some extent this process may happen naturally. Let us imagine a church, for example, where a good number of people have become Christians through a new 'Open Door'. These new Christians will have friends who may be interested as a result. The church may have had to rely until now on an Institutional fringe, but now it has acquired a Personal fringe, some of whom will be quite open. It will be important to provide suitable opportunities for bringing these friends. The results may be reflected in a growing 'basics' or enquirers' group. In such cases, changing the style to that of an Alpha Course (see chapter 8) may provide an opportunity for switching the emphasis from the Institutional to the Personal fringe.

This brings us to the third key question which needs to be asked. Is there an appropriate form of Persuasion evangelism in place? Without it, a church is like a football team without a striker. There may be complex and wonderful midfield manoeuvres, but they will not result in goals. The approach chosen will need, above all, to be suited to any plans for a new Open Door or Web strategy, as well as to the general needs of the church. In my own situation, I see it as a very high priority to introduce Good News Down the Street, one reason being that I believe it will be the most helpful approach for our baptism couples.

These are not the only questions, of course, which need to be asked. They are simply ones I should like to underline. Ideally, all areas of evangelism should be considered if the eventual strategy is to take account of all options. The reader may find that chapters 5 to 11 cover much of the ground, but naturally they are not exhaustive.

PRAYER AND PRIORITIES

Making a list of options will probably need to be done by the minister and one or two key leaders. Involvement in subsequent prayer and discussion will certainly need to be wider. How wide will depend on how major the changes are likely to be. In some cases it could be covered by the church council and the prayer meeting; in others it might require discussion by the home groups or even a special church conference. Debate could be assisted by those involved reading some common material – either a book such as this one, or else suitable material from the relevant denominational evangelism adviser. However the discussion is organized, neither the analytical nor the spiritual must be ignored. We have a responsibility to use our minds, but also to be sensitive to God's Spirit who may overrule our human thinking.

After prayer and discussion, the list may look very different. Some ideas will have to be discarded. Others will be 'green lights'. The largest group may be possibles for a future date. It has been wisely said that most of us overestimate what can be achieved in one year, but underestimate what can be achieved in 5 years.

Evangelism That Really Works

This book is offered in a spirit of enquiry. The author has tried to stick to approaches where he has found evidence that they really work. Nevertheless, where answers are given, they are not intended as final ones. The Spirit of God is on the move. New methods will arise.

I have presented some models (see chapter 13) which I hope will form a small contribution to the language we use for talking about evangelism. I would be sorry if they were ignored. I would be even more sorry if they were 'set in stone'. The reader should feel completely free to amend and improve the models. Even now the Holy Spirit may be prompting you to see that some different dynamic is operating in your church.

I would welcome comments and new insights, particularly from those at the cutting edge in different cultures or in different church traditions from my own. We need to learn from each other.

May God bless you and your church. May God encourage you as you carry out evangelism that really works.

APPENDICES

Appendix 1
Contents of the
Two Main Surveys

References in brackets are to the analysis in Appendix 2.

First Survey

1 Name of church and denomination (Table A1)
2 Type of community
3 Congregational details
4 Average Sunday attendance
5 Number of new adult Christians over 5 years (Table A2)
6 Size of fringe
7 Evangelistic impact of community groups (Table A3)
8 Impact of evangelistic and social events (Table A4)
9 Family services (Table A5)
10 First contact (Table A6)
11 Evangelism factors (Table A7)

Second Survey

The second survey omitted questions 8, 10 and 11, but included an additional question asking respondents to classify their church as belonging to one or more of the categories of Osmosis Model, Open Door, Web and Stepping-Stones (Table A8).

Appendix 2
Analysis of the Surveys

Table A1 Denomination and Churchmanship of Respondents

	First Survey	Second Survey	Total	
Response rate	*40%*	*41%*		
Anglicans				
Catholic, broad, liberal[1]	2	16	18	
Evangelical	17	11	28	
	19	27		46
Roman Catholic	0	10		10
Methodist[2]				
Broad, liberal	3	6	9	
Evangelical	2	2	4	
	5	8		13
Church of Scotland (both evangelical)	2	0		2
Baptist				
Evangelical	12	9	21	
Other	0	1	1	
	12	10		22
URC/Congregational				
Broad, liberal	0	5	5	
Evangelical	4	1	5	
	4	6		10
Pentecostal (evangelical)	2	0		2
Independent (evangelical)	4	5		9
	48	66		114

Notes 1. Too many respondents described themselves as both catholic and broad or liberal to differentiate in the analysis.
2. Including one Church of the Nazarene.

Table A2   Number of New Committed Christians

Women	1696	(61%)
Men	1066	(39%)
Total	2762	

101 churches completed this question. Thus, on average, each church had 27 new Christians over the 5-year period, or 5 per year. This compares with 3 public professions of faith per year in the CTE Research.

Table A3   Community Groups

Number of groups from 113 churches analysed according to effectiveness in fulfilling their evangelistic potential:

	Evangelistic Impact					Evangelism Not an Aim	Total
	None	Little	Adequate	Good	Unclear		
Parent and toddler	5	23	21	21	4	4	78
Senior citizens	6	12	25	12	3	3	61
Men's groups	2	8	7	5	1	6	29
Other women's groups	0	5	4	5	2	1	17
Total	13	48	57	43	10	14	185

Table A4   Evangelistic and Social Events and Guest Services

This question was not included in the second survey. The results below
were submitted by 34 churches.

	Frequency (No. of Churches)				Average Number of Adult Visitors
	Monthly	Every 2 to 5 Months	6-monthly or More	Total	
Adult guest services*	2	6	5	13	17
Guest family services	1	14	1	16	17
Evangelistic events with speaker	0	3	9	12	20
Social events with outsiders	3	12	9	24	30

	Evangelistic Impact (No. of Churches)				
	None	Little	Adequate	Good	Not Given, or Aim Not Evangelism
Adult guest services*	0	6	4	3	0
Guest family services	0	6	6	4	0
Evangelistic events with speaker	0	5	3	2	2
Social events with outsiders	1	8	8	4	3

* Excluding annual carol service (100 visitors) and annual memorial service for the departed (up to 50).

Table A5   All-Age Family Services

Frequency and Timing	No. of Churches	Average Attendance			
		Adults	Children	Uniformed Adult Fringe[1]	Other Adult Fringe
Monthly, at normal service time[2]	67	108	49	18	6[3]
Monthly, at different service time	2	45	30	5	31
Weekly	5	108	49	n/a	n/a
No family service[4]	40				
Total	114				

Notes: 1. Parents and leaders of uniformed organizations in the 39 churches for which the family service is also a parade.
2. Includes small number at other frequency than monthly, e.g., bimonthly.
3. Reduces to 3 if the 11 churches with the largest adult fringe are excluded.
4. The 10 Roman Catholic churches are included in this figure. Children are included in most Catholic services, and it is hard to differentiate all–age services, or to estimate the size of the fringe.

Table A6   First Contact

The following estimates of the ways new Christians were first contacted were from 43 of the 48 churches in the first survey and are in respect of 1,037 new Christians. This does not quite tally with the total number of adults contacted, 1,154, since some churches quite correctly listed more than one source of contact for some people.

	No. of Adults Contacted		
	Women	*Men*	*Total*
Already attended your church regularly	41	21	62
Long-term 'fringe' (occasional attender at services)	33	21	54
Simply came to a service	50	35	85
Drawn in by family service	57	32	89
Infant baptism/dedication contact	56	38	94
Bereavement contact	23	7	30
Wedding contact	14	11	25
Door-to-door visiting	12	3	15
Open-air work	2	2	4
Parent and toddler group	49	0	49
Pram service	0	0	0
Senior citizens' group	14	1	15
Parents of Scouts, Guides, etc.	5	2	7
Other community groups	23	5	28
Brought by friend*	198	114	312
Brought by family*	113	92	205
Neighbours/general community contact	21	12	33
Other (including church plant)	31	16	47
Total	742	412	1,154

* Split between friends and family allocated on the basis of 25 churches.

The proportion of the new Christians for whom first visit was to a service was as follows:

Men – 74%   Women – 70%

These figures are an average based on 34 churches. The percentage varied greatly, from 0 to 100%.

Table A7   Evangelism Factors

As in table A6, the following estimates are from returns from 43 churches.

A judgement had to be made as to which factors should be included under 'first contact', and which under 'evangelism'. Men's groups and social events were included under the latter since most of those invited would have some other source, particularly friends or family, as the first contact. Community groups were included under 'first contact' as a lower proportion of their members would already be friends, etc. of church members.

	No. of Adults Helped		
	Women	Men	Total
Specific help by friend/family	141	97	238
Helped by minister/leadership group	60	48	108
Personal evangelism using particular scheme (e.g. Evangelism Explosion)	10	5	15
General church involvement, services, etc.	79	59	138
Guest or special service(s)	116	73	189
Home events (supper parties, video evenings, etc.)	14	9	23
Other evangelistic events (your church)	2	0	2
City-wide, etc. evangelistic events	5	2	7
Men's group or events	0	21	21
Family social or evangelistic events (fun days, holiday clubs, etc.)	22	12	34
Other social events	51	30	81
'Power evangelism' (healing, dreams, etc.)	9	8	17
Personal Bible study	5	1	6
Home Bible study with church member(s) (Good News Down the Street, etc.)	98	61	159
Enquirers'/'basics'/catechumenate groups	80	43	123
Bible study/home groups – evening	14	11	25
– women's (day)	24	0	24
Other	10	5	15
Total	740	485	1,225

Table A8 Evangelization Models

For the first survey, the classification of churches by model was deduced from the overall questionnaire, particularly from the questions on the type of community, size of fringe, and methods of evangelization. For the second survey, the results were provided directly by an extra question (see Appendix 1).

	Number of Churches		
	First Survey	Second Survey	Total
Osmosis	5	25	30
Open Door	4	14	18
Web	6	5	11
Stepping-Stone	4	4	8
Osmosis/Open Door	4	5	9
Web/Stepping-Stone	0	3	3
Osmosis/Stepping-Stone	0	2	2
Open Door/Web	2	3	5
Open Door/Stepping-Stone	1	3	4
Osmosis/Web	1	1	2
Unclear	21	1	22
Total	48	66	114

Analysis of the comparative effectiveness of the models is contained in chapter 13.

Appendix 3
Mathematical
Growth Model

A Model of Church Growth Generated Through the Personal Fringe

1. Membership (N) = N (previous year) + C + J − L

   where C is number of converts
   J is number of joiners
   L is number of leavers

2. Membership (N) = N_o + N_n

   Subscripts

   o = old members (Christian >1 year)

   n = new members (Christian <1 year)

3. Conversions in year (C) = C_o + C_n

   $$= N_o n_o p_o r_o + N_n n_n p_n r_n$$

   where N = number of adult congregation

   n = number of unchurched friends, etc. per person

   p = proportion of friends in local community

   r = proportion receptive to the gospel

The following simplifying assumptions are made:

   a. Those who are receptive to the gospel will become Christians if they have a committed Christian friend from the church and also live in the catchment area
   b. biological growth = deaths
   c. number converted through the clergy = committed folk who lapse

Appendix 4
Growth Model – Worked Example

In appendix 4 we work through an example using the growth model in appendix 3. Let us first consider two churches which are similar in most respects.

Church A starts with a congregation of 100 of which 5 are new Christians. Five existing Christians transfer to the church each year. The annual number who leave is equal to 10% of the established Christians.

The established Christians have an average of 10 friends and family who are not Christians. Of these, 20% live in the catchment area of the church. The proportion of them who are receptive to Christian faith is only 2%.

The new Christians have a larger number of unchurched friends, averaging 20 each. Of these, likewise, 20% live in range of the church. A higher proportion are open to Christian faith for reasons suggested in chapter 12, averaging 10%.

The only difference for church B is that 40%, rather than 20% of friends live in the catchment area of the church. It is a slightly less scattered community.

These data can be summarized, using the nomenclature of appendix 3, as follows:

	Established Christians	New Christians
n	10	20
p (church A)	0.2	0.2
p (church B)	0.4	0.4
r	0.02	0.1

$J = 5 \qquad L = 0.1 \, N_o$

Using the data in the table, equation 3 in appendix 3 becomes:

Church A
$$C = C_o + C_n = 0.04 \, N_o + 0.4 \, N_n$$

Church B
$$C = C_o + C_n = 0.08 \, N_o + 0.8 \, N_n$$

Using the 3 equations in appendix 3, the growth in membership of the two churches can now be calculated. It will be seen from table A9 that church A remains fairly static, while church B experiences dramatic growth.

We now introduce church C where, as well as there being a higher proportion of friends in the catchment area, the friends are also twice as receptive to the gospel (or, alternatively, the Christians have twice as many friends – or a mixture of both.) Equation 3 then becomes:

Church C
$$C = C_o + C_n = 0.16 \, N_o + 1.6 \, N_n$$

The assumption does not seem unreasonable, yet it will be seen that the resultant growth is meteoric, with the congregation growing to more than 12,000 in 12 years.

Table A9   Comparative Church Growth

Church A

Year	N	N_o	N_n	C_o	C_n	J	L
1	100	95	5	4	2	5	9
2	102	96	6	4	2	5	9
3	104	98	6	4	2	5	9
4	106	100	6	4	2	5	10
5	107	101	6	4	2	5	10
6	108	102	6	4	2	5	10
7	109	103	6	4	2	5	10
8	110	104	6	4	2	5	10
9	111	105	6	4	2	5	10
10	112	106	6	4	2	5	10
11	113	107	6	4	2	5	10
12	114	108	6	4	2	5	10
13	115	109	6	4	2	5	10
14	116	110	6	4	2	5	11
15	116			Plateau			

Table A9 (continued)

Church B

Year	N	N_o	N_n	C_o	C_n	J	L
1	100	95	5	8	4	5	9
2	108	96	12	8	10	5	9
3	122	104	18	8	14	5	10
4	139	117	22	9	18	5	11
5	160	133	27	11	22	5	13
6	185	152	33	12	26	5	15
7	213	175	38	14	30	5	17
8	245	201	44	16	35	5	20
9	281	230	51	18	41	5	23
10	322	263	59	21	47	5	26
11	369	301	68	24	54	5	30
12	422	344	78	28	62	5	34
13	483	393	90	31	72	5	39
14	552	449	103	36	82	5	44
15	631	513	118				

Church C

Year	N	N_o	N_n	C_o	C_n	J	L
1	100	95	5	15	8	5	9
2	119	96	23	15	37	5	10
3	166	114	52	18	83	5	11
4	261	160	101	26	161	5	16
5	437	250	187	40	299	5	25
6	756	417	339	67	542	5	42
7	1,328	719	609	115	974	5	72
8	2,350	1,261	1,089	202	1,742	5	126
9	4,173	2,229	1,944	357	3,110	5	223
10	7,422	3,955	3,467	633	5,547	5	395
11	13,212	7,032	6,180				

Notes

Chapter 1
1. Pope Paul VI, *Evangelization in the Modern World* (Catholic Truth Society 1975), section 14.
2. Results published in Finney, J.T., *Finding Faith Today* (Bible Society 1992), p. 6.
3. Abraham, W.J., *The Logic of Evangelism* (Hodder & Stoughton 1989), pp. 40ff.
4. Stott, J.R.W., *The Lausanne Covenant: An Exposition and Commentary* (Minneapolis, World Wide Publications 1975), p. 20.
5. Abraham, *The Logic of Evangelism*, pp. 46ff.
6. Pope Paul VI, *Evangelization in the Modern World*, section 18.
7. Pointer, R., *How Do Churches Grow?* (MARC Europe and British Church Growth Association), pp. 64ff.

Chapter 2
1. See, for example, Fowler, J.W., *Stages of Faith: The Psychology of Human Development and the Quest for Meaning* (San Francisco, Harper & Row 1981), and Westerhoff, J.H., *Will Our Children Have Faith?* (New York, Seabury Press 1976).
2. Finney, *Finding Faith Today*, p. 24.
3. Pointer, *How Do Churches Grow?*, p. 193.
4. Robb, J.D., *FOCUS! The Power of People Group Thinking* (MARC Europe 1989), p. 44.
5. I am thinking of the unhelpful 'coincidences' that can occur when someone starts to show an interest in Christian faith. I think, for example, of a man who finally plucked up courage to come to my house, which was only 100 yards away. In that short distance he was stopped by Jehovah's Witnesses and given a video!
6. Ecclesiastes 4.12 (NIV).
7. Acts 2.41.
8. For example, Jeremiah 23.29; John 15.7.
9. Hanley, P., *Finding Faith Today Technical Report* (Bible Society 1992), p. 71. See also Finney, *Finding Faith Today*, pp. 43ff.
10. Finney, *Finding Faith Today*, p. 44.
11. Luke 22.32.
12. This concept was first put forward by Ralph Winter.
13. Hanley, *Finding Faith Today Technical Report*, and Finney, *Finding Faith Today*.

Chapter 3

1. McGavran, D.A., *Understanding Church Growth* (3rd edn., revised Wagner, C.P., Eerdmans 1990), p. 261.

Chapter 5

1. For example, Wigley, J., *Under Fives and Their Families* (Marshall Pickering 1990), and also Wigley, J., *Reaching Young Families* (CPAS 1994).
2. Church Pastoral Aid Society (CPAS) Families and Under Fives Ministry, Athena Drive, Tachbrook Park, Warwick CV34 6NG.
3. Breen, M., *Outside In* (Scripture Union 1993).

Chapter 6

1. Sherwin, D.R., *A Prayer-Evangelism Strategy* (Grove Booklet Ev. 26, 1994).
2. c/o Release Publications, Manchester City Mission, Windsor Church and Youth Centre, Churchill Way, Salford M6 5AU.
3. Bradbury, N., *City of God? Pastoral Care in the Inner City* (SPCK 1989), pp. 177–92, 199.

Chapter 7

1. Finney, *Finding Faith Today*, p. 46.
2. From a case study in *Good News*, a broadsheet issued by the Church of England's Board of Mission, October 1993 edn.
3. Finney, *Finding Faith Today*, p. 27.
4. Dalby, M., *Open Baptism* (SPCK 1989) and Buchanan, C.O. *A Case for Infant Baptism* (Grove Booklet, P20, 4th edn 1989).
5. Buchanan, C.O., *Infant Baptism and the Gospel* (Darton, Longman and Todd 1993).
6. Wooderson, M., *The Church Down Our Street* (MARC 1989), p. 169.
7. *Good News for You*, a video introducing Good News Down the Street.
8. Wooderson, *The Church Down Our Street*, p. 143.
9. See, for example, Robinson, M., *A World Apart* (Monarch 1992), and also Hill, M., *Reaching the Unchurched* (Scripture Press 1994).

Chapter 8

1. Details from Evangelism Explosion National Office, 228 Shirley Road, Southampton SO1 3HR.
2. Wooderson, M., *Good News Down the Street* (Grove Booklet P9, 4th edn 1994). This and other helpful materials from: The Network Trust, 100 Lazy Hill Road, Aldridge, Walsall, West Midlands WS9 8RR.
3. *The Rite of Christian Initiation of Adults* copyright © 1985 International Committee on English in the Liturgy Inc. (ICEL).
4. See, for example, Ball, R., *Adult Believing* (Mowbray 1988).
5. I based this on an unpublished study of 26 catechumenate groups carried out by Captain David Sanderson of the Church Army.
6. For details of other conferences and helpful books, tapes and videos contact: Alpha Course, Holy Trinity Brompton, Brompton Road, London SW7 1JA.
7. Simmons, P., *Reaching the Unchurched: Some Lessons from Willow Creek* (Grove Booklet Ev.19, 1992).

8. Holy Trinity, Brompton's advice is to try the Alpha Course in its proven format before experimenting.
9. Finney, *Finding Faith Today*, p. 38.
10. *Open House Magazine* (CPAS 1992), number 20.
11. Nicky Gumbel speaking at the HTB Alpha course conference in May 1993.

Chapter 9

1. Jeremiah 23.29 (NIV).
2. Finney, *Finding Faith Today*, p. 68.
3. *Take a Closer Look at the Claims of Christ* (Nelson Word 1994).

Chapter 10

1. Brierley, P., *Christian England* (MARC Europe 1991), p. 79.
2. See, for example, Wakefield, G., *Where Are the Men?* (Grove Booklet P34, 1988).
3. Christian Viewpoint for Men, Townsend Chambers, Amherst Hill, Sevenoaks, Kent TN13 2EL.
4. See, for example, Browne, L., *Sport and Recreation Evangelism in the Local Church* (Grove Booklet Ev.13, 1991).
5. *Church of England Newspaper* (November 1993).

Chapter 11

1. Neighbour, R.W. Jr, *The Shepherd's Guidebook* (Houston, Touch Publications 1988).
2. Time Ministries International, Emmanuel Church, Main Road, Hawkwell, Hockley, Essex SS5 4NR.

Chapter 12

1. Wasdell, D., *Let My People Grow!* (Urban Church Project Workpaper number 1, 1974).
2. Though see Wasdell, *Let My People Grow!* p. 8.
3. Wasdell, *Let My People Grow!* p. 9.

Chapter 13

1. The 75% quartile means the 25th largest church in a sample of 100 churches.
2. Lynch, P., *Awakening the Giant* (Darton, Longman and Todd 1990).

Chapter 14

1. Warren, R., *On the Anvil* (Highland Books 1990).
2. Warren, *On the Anvil*, p. 55.
3. See, for example, *Mission Audit* (Board for Mission and Unity 1984), and also Finney, J.T., *The Well Church Book* (CPAS 1991).

Index of Churches and Organizations

General Index